Equity Finance

EQUITY FINANCE

Brian Coyle

FINANCIAL
WORLD
Publishing
THE CHARTERED INSTITUTE OF BANKERS

Financial World Publishing
IFS House
4-9 Burgate Lane
Canterbury
Kent
CT1 2XJ
United Kingdom

Telephone: 01227 818687

Financial World Publishing publications are published by
The Chartered Institute of Bankers, a non-profit making registered educational charity.

Typeset by Kevin O'Connor
Printed in Italy

ISBN 0-85297-453-1

Contents

Features of Equity

The term equity describes the ownership of a company. Ownership is represented by shares that give their holder a part or a share of the enterprise. Equity shares are called various names, common stock in the US and mainly ordinary shares elsewhere.

Equity also includes instruments that give their holder the right to subscribe for common stock in the company at some time in the future. Both share options issued by a company and share warrants give their holders this right. Options and warrants can be described as delayed equity because they might be used to create new equity shares, but not until some time in the future.

There is also a view that convertible bonds and convertible preferred stocks are equity. These give their holders the right to convert the bonds or preferred stock into equity shares of the company at a future date, at a specified fixed rate of conversion. If the holders of the convertibles exercise their right of conversion, the company must issue new ordinary shares.

Many corporate treasurers and stock-market analysts would argue that irredeemable preferred stocks are also a form of equity because they are part of the permanent share capital of the company.

The definition of equity is not clear-cut, and some securities and instruments are more properly regarded as hybrids, part-debt and part-equity.

Equity

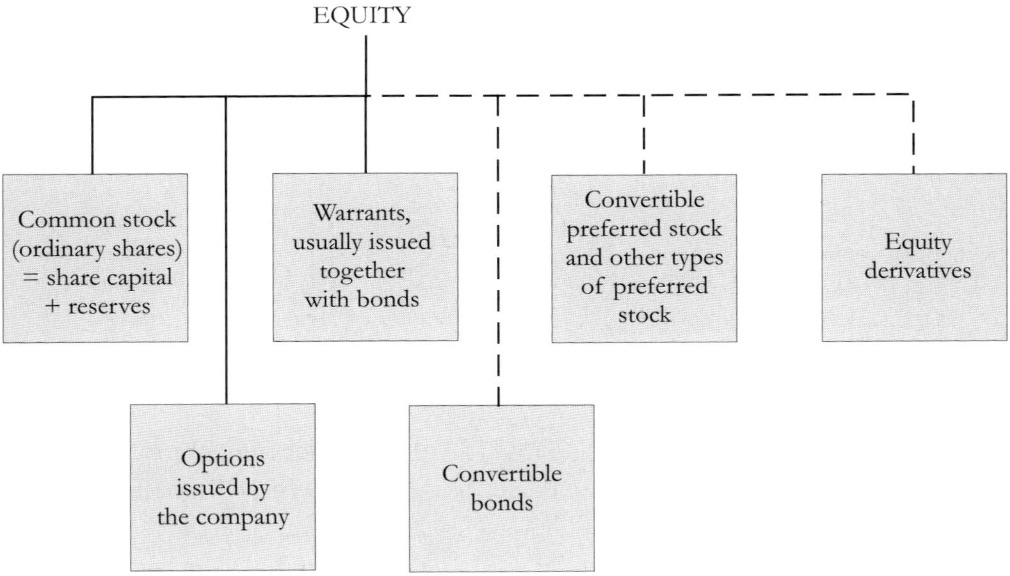

There are also equity derivatives. These are derivative instruments, equity futures and equity options, that are used to make equity-related transactions without buying or selling any equity shares.

Equity Investment

The equity investment in a company is represented, in accounting terms, within its balance sheet. Equity capital is the net worth of the company, consisting of its total assets minus its liabilities to creditors and other providers of capital, i.e. the net assets of the business.

In a balance sheet, equity capital is represented by the ordinary share capital at nominal value, and the reserves, such as the share premium account, revaluation reserve and retained-profits account.

Balance Sheet Contents

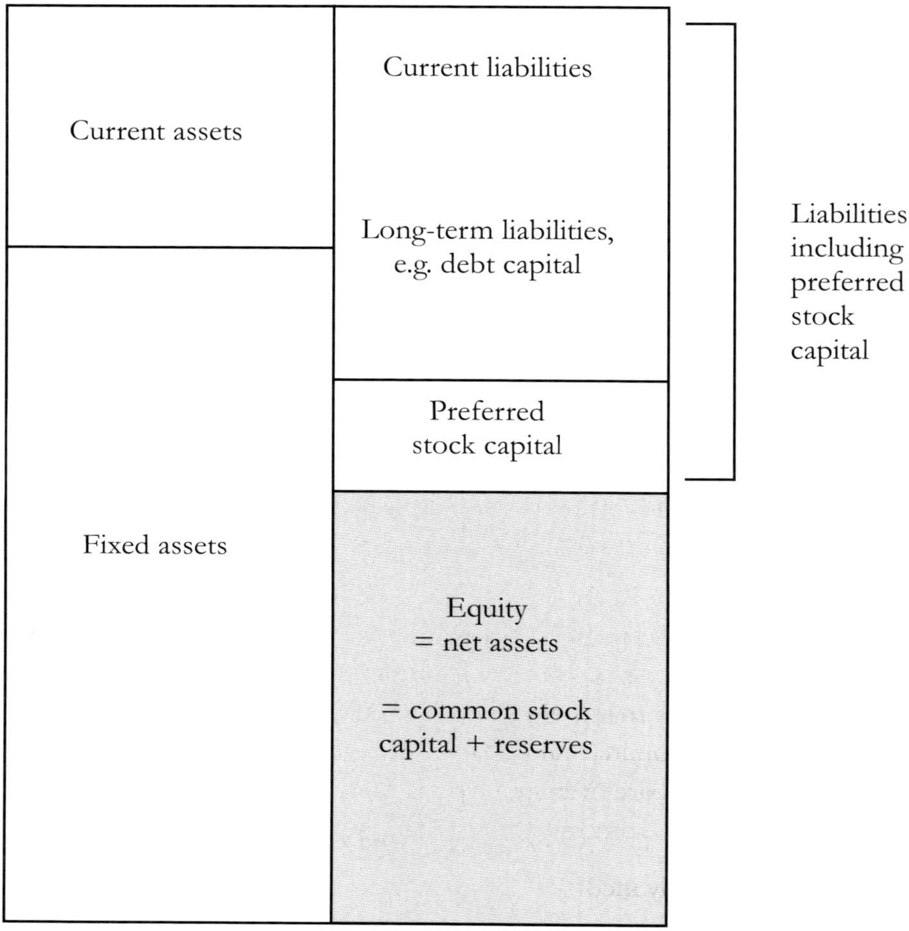

However, the accounting valuation of assets, particularly fixed assets, is notoriously unreliable, and the equity investment in a company cannot be measured reliably by balance-sheet values.

Limited Liability

The net assets of a company represent what the equity shareholders own and also the limit of their investment risk. The liability of shareholders to the creditors of their company is limited to the amount of capital they have already subscribed. If a company is forced into liquidation with debts that it cannot afford to pay, the shareholders will not be required to put up extra money to settle the debts provided the shares are fully paid with respect to their nominal value.

The concept of limited liability is a legal one, but it has relevance to equity investments. If a company went into liquidation, an investor in the equity shares of a company cannot lose more than the cost of his/her original investment.

Nominal Value and Issue Price

All shares have a nominal value or face value. All shares in the same class must have the same nominal value that is usually a convenient round figure amount.

The issue price of shares need not be their nominal value, and often will be an amount in excess of the nominal value. When new shares are issued by a company that is already established, the issue price invariably is higher than the nominal value. The excess of the issue price over the nominal value is a share premium, and is reported in the balance sheet in a share-premium account as part of the equity capital of the company.

Suppose that a newly incorporated company issues 50,000 shares of $1.

- The issue price must be at least $1 per share, the nominal value, although the company can choose to call up the money in instalments.
- If the issue price is higher, for example $3, the company would raise $150,000, of which $50,000 would be reported in the balance sheet as share capital, and the remaining $100,000 would be reported as share premium.

All shares in the same class rank equally, regardless of the price at which they were issued. If, for example, a company issues common stock in

Year 1 at $1.50 each, and makes a further issue of common stock in Year 4 at $5 per share, the shares will rank equally; for example, the company would pay the same dividend on all the shares.

Voting Power

An equity shareholding gives the shareholder a right to vote at general meetings of the company. Voting power is relative to the size of the shareholding. Management control of a company, however, is in the hands of the board of directors. Shareholders can exert control or a strong influence over their company:

- when they own more than 50% of the voting shares
- when they have one or more representatives on the board of directors, or
- when they are directors of the company.

Minority shareholders can have very little influence on how their company is run, despite their voting rights, particularly when the company is controlled by a majority shareholder.

Classes of Shares

In some companies, equity shares are divided into two or more classes, each with differing voting rights. Some companies have a class of common stock that have no voting rights at all. The purpose of non-voting equity usually is to limit voting powers to a smaller group of shareholders who thereby retain control of the company with less than 50% of its common stock capital. The prevalence of different classes of common stock varies between countries.

What Form Do Shares Take?

Traditionally shares have been issued as certificates. Each certificate represents ownership of a stated quantity of shares in the company. Many stock markets now provide investors with the opportunity, permitted by changes in company law, to hold shares as computer entries in book-entry form in a stock account with a recognized organization known as a central securities depository. When shares are held in book-entry form, there need not be an underlying certificate, and the shares therefore are uncertificated.

Shares, whether issued as certificates or in book-entry form, are either:

- bearer shares, or
- registered shares.

Bearer Shares

Possession of bearer shares in certificate form gives its holder legal title to the shares. Each certificate is for a stated quantity, usually a round number of shares. The owner's name does not appear on the certificate, and ownership can be transferred simply by giving the certificate to the buyer.

Bearer share certificates are issued with a number of coupons or talons. Each coupon is an entitlement to receive an interim or final dividend in a particular year. To claim a dividend, the shareholder or his/her agent must detach the appropriate coupon and present it to the company's paying agent, usually a bank, for payment at the appropriate time.

Bearer shares are the usual form of shares in some countries, particularly in continental Europe.

When bearer shares are held in book-entry form, ownership is evidenced by the computer record. Dividends are paid by the company to the central securities depository that transfers the money to the investor.

Registered Shares

Ownership and any transfer of ownership of registered shares is recorded in an official register of shareholders that may be maintained for the company by a company specializing in the provision of a registrar's service. Legal title to the shares is determined by the entry in the share register.

When registered shares are in certificate form, the name of the shareholder and the exact number of shares held, that need not be a convenient round number, is shown on the face of the share certificate. When registered shares are held with a central securities depository in computer form, the company's registrar has a computer link to the depository. Purchases or sales of shares by account holders with the depository are notified to the registrar by message transfer.

Dividends are paid on registered shares to the owner whose name is on the register at a given date. For example, a company might pay a final dividend for its financial year to December 31 on April 29 to shareholders whose names are on the shareholders' register at the close of business several weeks earlier, on March 1st for example. The reason for establishing a cut-off date for dividend payments is simply an administrative one. It takes time to record a change of share ownership in the shareholders' register, and it is appropriate to establish an official last day for trading in the shares cum dividend, i.e. with rights to the next dividend belonging to the buyer of the shares.

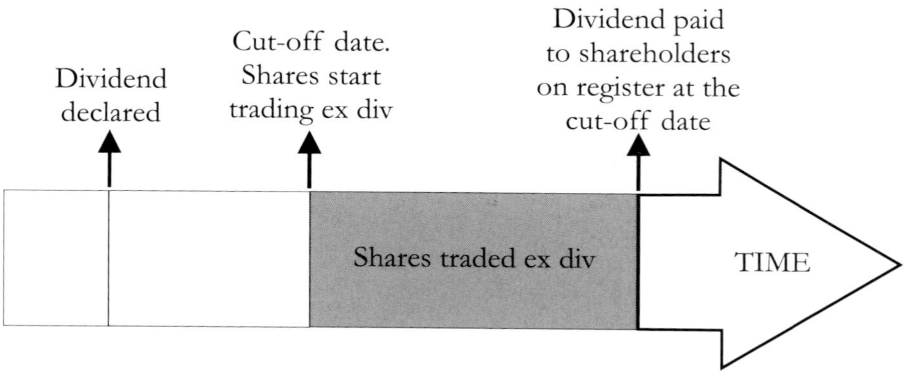

If registered shares in a company are sold after a cut-off date for a dividend has passed but before the dividend payment date has been reached, they are traded ex dividend. The seller of the shares whose name is on the register at the cut-off date, receives the next dividend payment. When shares traded on a stock market enter an ex-dividend period for trading, the share price is quoted ex div, with the symbol xd after the share price, e.g. 461 xd.

Registered shares are used in several countries, notably the US, UK and Japan.

Uncertificated Shares: Book-Entry Systems

Share certificates can create a large amount of administrative work, particularly for registered shares. When registered shares are transferred to a new owner, at least one new certificate and often two or even more, must be issued. For example, suppose that Alpha owns 50,000 shares in a company and sells 20,000 of these shares to Beta. Alpha will surrender its share certificate for 50,000 shares. The company's registrar must then issue two new certificates, one to Alpha for the remaining 30,000 shares and one to Beta for 20,000 shares.

There are problems too with bearer shares in certificate form. Because physical possession gives a person legal title to the shares, there is a real risk of losing certificates, or having certificates stolen. Large institutional investors leave their bearer certificates with a bank or depository for safekeeping. The investor might never see the certificates, even when they are sold and if the buyer of bearer shares uses the same depository for safekeeping, the certificates will not be moved, but will stay in the same location. Institutional investors do not need certificates, and find them inconvenient.

To reduce the effort and the cost of maintaining a share register, the stock markets in various countries have developed computerized systems for computerized book-entry records of share ownership. Ownership is recorded on a computer file, in a stock account for the investor, and no share certificates are issued. Transfers of ownership between investors with a stock account in the system can be made simply by computer entry.

For a book-entry system to be feasible, there are several requirements.

- The holding of shares in computerized form, without a certificate, must be permitted by the national laws of the country where the company is incorporated.
- There has to be recognized organizations that operate a book-entry system of share ownership. Recognition has to be provided either by legislation or by the government's regulator of the stock markets. If more than one organization is permitted to operate a book-entry system for the same stock market, these should have computer links between each other for recording transfers of ownership. Without such links, a book-entry system of share ownership might be inefficient.

Book-entry systems for share ownership and transfers of ownership are operated by several central securities depositories around the world. These include the Depository Trust Company in the US, part of the Depository Trust and Clearing Corporation, Clearstream and Euroclear in continental Europe, and Crest in the UK. Users of these systems must be participants in the system or members of the organization operating the system.

When bearer shares are in *certificate form*, investment institutions and large private investors may lodge their share certificates with a custodian for safekeeping. The custodian can be a depository such as Clearstream or Euroclear. The records of share ownership, and transfers of ownership, then can be recorded by book-entry, without the share certificate having to be moved.

Nominee Accounts for Shareholding

Shareholders may hold registered shares in their own name. It might be convenient, however, to arrange for someone else to hold the shares on the investor's behalf. This person will receive the dividends on the shares, which he/she will then pass on to the investor. The holder also will enjoy all the other entitlements of the shareholder, such as the right to vote at meetings of the company.

Organizations that hold shares on behalf of other investors hold them as street names or as nominees outside the US. For example, a firm of stockbrokers might hold registered shares on behalf of several clients, and use street names, each client having a separate account. The name of the registered owner of the shares in the company's share register, will be the street name. Alternatively, the broker might keep just one street name in which it holds all the shares of all its clients. However, it would have to ensure that the shareholdings of each client were kept segregated and properly recorded.

Such accounts also are used within book-entry systems for registered shares. The only organizations permitted to maintain a computerized stock account are participants in the system, such as investment banks, large institutional investors and some firms of brokers and dealers. Anyone else wanting to hold shares in book-entry form would have to arrange for a system participant to hold the shares on his/her behalf. The shares can be held by the participant in a street name account as a distinct sub-account within its overall stock account in the system.

Custody

Some organizations, such as some banks, offer a custody service to large institutional investors. A custody service involves taking over the administration of the client's investment portfolio, including making sure the securities are kept safely, collecting interest and dividends on behalf of the client, and arranging for the settlement of stockmarket transactions by the client, delivering the securities, making the payment. Some custodians operate nationally and look after all the client's securities that have been issued by organizations in that country. A few organizations operate a global custody service that involves the administration of the client's worldwide investments. A global custodian might use the services of national custodians if it does not have its own custody operations in a particular country or part of the world.

Dividends

Equity shareholders have a right to a dividend from the profits of the company, but only if a dividend is declared by the board of directors. Dividends are dealt with in the next chapter.

Conclusion

Retained profits are by far the most important source of new equity. By comparison, many companies do not raise much capital by issuing new shares in the equities markets. The equity markets are nevertheless important.

- They can be a source of funding for a public company that wants to raise capital in the form of cash.
- Without a secondary market for their shares, shareholders could struggle to find a buyer for their shares when they want to sell their investment. A liquid secondary market in a company's shares allows a shareholder to realize his/her investment by selling shares at any time at a fair price.
- The stock market price at which shares are traded can provide a reasonable guide to the current value of the company's equity, and indicate to an investor how well or badly the investment is performing. Many companies acknowledge that their prime objective is to maximize the wealth of their equity shareholders. Consequently the performance of a company can be judged by a combination of its dividend payments and changes in its share price.

Equity funding has a number of advantages for companies, notably its permanence. Common stocks represent permanent capital. They are perpetual unless the company decides it should buy back some of its shares for cancellation. Raising long-term capital in the form of equity therefore is a low-risk option for a company, in the sense that it is not exposed to any refinancing risk of the kind that can occur with debt capital. Refinancing risk is the possibility that a company will be unable to raise new capital to replace existing capital that is reaching maturity and redemption.

As a general rule, equity has a higher cost than debt capital, particularly in the long term, because equity shareholders usually require dividend growth. Equity has an adjustable cost, however, because companies can vary the annual dividend up or down each year, according to what they can afford. Some start-up companies, for example those in e-commerce, might not be expected to pay dividends for several years after being set up. In such cases, investors are prepared to forgo dividends in the short term in the expectation of significant long-term dividend income.

Equity is far less restrictive than debt capital. Bank loans and issues of debt securities invariably have covenants attached that restrict the company's financial flexibility until the debt is repaid. For example, covenants could set minimum thresholds for financial gearing, net worth, current ratio and interest cover. The company must comply with its covenants or go into default and be required to repay the loan or renegotiate its terms with the lender.

Equity by contrast carries no restrictive covenants. Once investors have subscribed for equity shares, they rely completely on the management of the company to use their investment wisely. The only course of action that might be available to them is to replace poorly performing management.

Equity Returns and Yields

Companies are expected to provide a return on the investment of their common stockholders. Returns for equity investors are measured in terms of:

- dividends and dividend yield
- dividends and share price growth, and
- profits and earnings per share.

The success of a company can be judged by the size and stability or growth trend of these returns. Equity returns also are assessed by comparing returns with the returns made by other companies.

Dividends

The return to equity shareholders during a period can be measured simply as the dividends per share paid by the company. Dividends are the cash received by shareholders, and are a direct and tangible return on investment.

Because equity shares are the permanent capital of a company, their value to an investor lies in the amount of all the future dividends that shareholders can expect to receive from their shares. A shareholder might eventually sell his/her shares, but the value of the shares to the buyer lies in the future expected dividends.

Companies normally declare or propose a dividend when they announce their profits for a period. It is usual for major US companies that announce profits quarterly, to pay a quarterly dividend. For similar reasons, most UK public companies pay their annual dividend in two stages. Occasionally, a UK public company pays a quarterly dividend. Some companies, particularly private companies, pay an annual dividend.

Dividends and Tax Credits

Dividends usually are paid in cash. The payment could be gross or net of a tax deduction, according to the tax regulations that apply. When a company makes a tax deduction, and pays this tax to the government, the tax deducted and paid is known as withholding tax.

Suppose for example that the tax rules in a particular country require companies to make a deduction of 20% from dividends they pay to shareholders, and to pay this to the government. If the company decided to pay a cash dividend of $8 million, it would be required to pay withholding tax of $2 million to the government. The gross dividend, consisting of cash dividend and tax credit, would be $10 million, of which 20% is paid in tax directly by the company to the government. A shareholder receiving a cash dividend of $4,000 would have earned gross income of $5,000 including the tax credit. The income tax required to be paid on the dividend will be the tax payable on $5,000, of which $10,000 has been already paid.

Dividend Yield

The annual dividend per share can be compared with the value of the investment, the current share price, and reported as a dividend yield. A dividend yield is simply a measure of income yield on investment.

$$\text{Dividend yield} = \frac{\text{Dividend x } 100\%}{\text{Current share price}}$$

Where the company deducts withholding tax, and all shareholders receive the same tax credit, the dividend figure might be the cash dividend plus the tax credit. This yield is called the gross dividend yield.

When there is no withholding tax, or where shareholders receive differing rates of tax credit, the dividend figure will be the cash dividend only. The dividend yield is then a net dividend yield.

The current share price is used to report dividend yield, although an individual investor might prefer to measure his/her income yield on the basis of the price originally paid for the shares. Using the current share price, however, has the benefits of:

- showing what income yield a new investor in the shares might expect to receive by buying shares in the company, and
- providing a fair basis for comparison of dividend yields between companies.

Example
A company's dividend for the past financial year consisted of an interim dividend of 10¢ per share and a final dividend of 17¢. The current share price is 830¢.

Analysis

$$\text{Dividend yield} = \frac{(10 + 17)}{820} \times 100\% = 3.3\%$$

Dividend yield normally is a historical measurement. The reported yield is based on dividends for the previous year. A prospective dividend yield could be calculated by making a forecast of what dividends for the current year will be.

When a company declares a quarterly dividend or an interim mid-year dividend, it is usual to continue reporting dividend yield on the basis of the total dividend for the previous year. The dividend yield is not updated to reflect the current year's interim or quarterly dividend amounts.

The size of dividend yield that equity shareholders expect varies between countries. Japanese companies, for example, have a very high ratio of share price to dividend, and dividend yields are very low. In the UK, average dividend yields currently are between 2% and 3%.

Dividend yields on a company's shares vary according to the investment risk, and depend as much on the share price as on the amount of dividend paid.

- Yields generally are lower for profitable companies than for companies in a depressed industry or with low profits. When the share price of a company collapses after the company announces a profits warning to the stock market, the dividend yield will go up. For example, if a company's share price falls by 50% after the announcement of a profits warning, its dividend yield will double in size.
- Yields are lower when the company's profits and dividends are expected to grow over time. Investors will pay more to buy the shares, and the current dividend yield will be low. In contrast, dividend yields on low-growth shares usually are relatively high.
- Yields generally are lower for public companies whose shares trade in a liquid secondary market than for smaller companies whose shares cannot be traded as easily. Investors require a higher yield to compensate them for the lack of liquidity in the shares, and also because the investment might be a bigger risk.

Equity investors usually expect dividends on their shares to increase over time, at least in step with price inflation. If dividends increase over time, it might be supposed that dividend yields also will rise. This is not the case. When dividends increase over time, the share price also will rise. Therefore dividend yield could remain stable, rising only slowly, or even falling.

Example
In Year 1, a company's dividend per share was 12¢ and its share price was 300¢. In the next year, the dividend went up to 13.6¢ per share, and the share price rose to 350¢.

Analysis
The dividend yield was originally 4% (12 ÷ 300 x 100%). In the next year, it fell to 3.9% (13.6 ÷ 350 x 100%). The fall in yield occurred because there was a 13.3% rise in dividend, but an even bigger percentage rise (16.7%) in the share price.

Scrip Dividend

Dividend occasionally is paid in the form of shares rather than cash. This form of dividend is known as a scrip dividend. Shareholders must approve a proposal by the board of directors to create new shares for this purpose, and are not forced to receive a dividend in shares. They can choose a cash alternative.

The dividend is declared as a money amount. A valuation is placed on each new share for the purpose of deciding the scrip dividend entitlement of each shareholder. This valuation, in the case of a listed company, will be its stockmarket price.

Example

A company declares a final dividend of 5¢ per share. Shareholders are given the option of a scrip dividend as an alternative to payment in cash. The issue price/value of each new share is 251.1¢, to reflect the current market price of the shares.

Analysis

Suppose that a holder of 10,000 shares in the company chose to receive the scrip dividend. The total dividend receivable would be $500 (10,000 x 5¢). The shareholder would receive 199 new shares as dividend with each share priced at 251.1¢ on issue ($500 ÷ 251.1¢ per share). These shares would be worth $499.69 (199 x 251.1¢) and the balance of the dividend due to the shareholder, 31¢, would be paid in cash.

Dividends and Share Price Growth

Dividends and dividend yield are not a wholly satisfactory measurement of return on equity during a period, because equity shareholders also benefit from any share price growth and suffer from any fall in share price. The total return on equity during a period could be measured as:

- the dividend
- plus any increase in share price, or minus any fall in share price.

The change in share price will reflect the revised expectations of investors about the *future* prospects of the company, rather than historical dividends.

Example

At the beginning of Year 1, a company's share price was 420¢. During the year, dividends per share were 20¢. At the end of the year, expectations about the company's prospects had improved and the share price was 500¢.

Analysis

The total return from dividends and share price growth is as follows:

	cents
Dividend	20
Share price growth (500 – 420)	80
	100

As a percentage of the start-of-year share price, the return to shareholders for the year was 23.8% (100/420). As a percentage of the end-of-year share price, the return was 20% (100/500). However, the dividend yield as at the year-end is only 4% (20/500). Most of the return has come from share price growth, and improved expectations for the future.

Profits and Earnings per Share (EPS)

The annual profits of a company that are attributable to equity shareholders are the profits after taxation and preferred stock dividends. Of these profits, some are paid to shareholders as dividends and the rest are retained in the business.

Retained profits that are a major source of capital for companies, can serve two purposes:

- to protect the erosion of the company's real assets against the effects of inflation. Profits reported by the historical cost-accounting convention ignore the effects of inflation. Some extra capital is needed, perhaps by retaining profits, to allow for the higher cost of asset replacements

- to reinvest capital in the business for future growth in profits and dividends.

Example
A company pays 40% of its after-tax profits in dividends. The remaining 60% is retained and reinvested. There is no inflation, and the return on new investment is 5%.

Analysis
By retaining 60% of its profits and reinvesting them to earn a 5% per annum return, the company can expect to achieve a growth in profits of 3% per annum (5% of 60%).

For example, suppose the company makes profits of $100 million and retains 60% for reinvestment. If the annual return on investment is 5%, the $60 million retained profits will add $3 million to total profits next year (5% of $60 million), thereby increasing total profits by 3%.

If the company maintains the 60% ratio of retained profits to total equity profits, and continues to reinvest at 5%, it would continue to achieve growth in profits and dividends of 3% per annum indefinitely.

Dividend Cover
Dividend cover is the ratio of equity profits for the year to the dividends declared out of those profits. Equity profits are profits after taxation and preferred dividends. For example, suppose that a company with no preferred stock capital made a profit after tax of $100 million, and dividends for the year were $40 million. The dividend cover would be 2.5 times ($100 million ÷ $40 million). Dividends are 40% of after-tax profits, and retained profits therefore are 60% of after-tax profits.

It is usual for companies to try to maintain a dividend cover of around 2.0 to 2.5 times and retain about 50% to 60% of profits. The ability to do this depends mainly on profit performance. Dividend cover below 1.5 to 2.0 times often has been considered low by investors and stock market analysts.

Dividend Cuts and Uncovered Dividend

Companies are allowed to pay dividends out of profits for the current year and also out of accumulated retained profits from previous years. Therefore dividends can be paid by a loss-making company, for example. When a company pays a dividend to common stockholders that exceeds current-year profits, it is said to be paying an uncovered dividend.

Companies try to achieve a steady growth in dividend payments from one year to the next, with the size of dividend ideally growing in line with, or higher than, the rate of inflation. However, if the company's profits fall sharply, it might have to consider the relative merits of cutting the dividend or maintaining the payout at the previous year's level, even though this would not be covered by the current year's profits. If the poor profits performance is considered by the directors to be a temporary setback because of one-off factors, such as high costs of rationalization or a short cyclical downturn in trading, the dividend might be maintained at the previous year's level.

The reason for paying an uncovered dividend primarily is to retain the goodwill of the major shareholders, particularly the institutional investors, many of whom rely on a stream of dividend income to meet their own financial obligations, including pension payments, insurance claims, etc.. When a company cuts its dividend, its runs the risk that institutional shareholders could respond by:

- selling their shares in the market, so depressing the share price
- lobbying or voting for a management change
- selling their shares to a bidder for the company, should a takeover bid occur.

US companies have tended to make cuts in dividend to reflect a decline in trading performance. Even so, the impact of a dividend cut by a top US company can be profound.

Earnings per Share

An important measure of equity performance is earnings per share (EPS). The exact definition of EPS can vary from one country to another.

Essentially, EPS is the profit attributable to common stockholders, divided by the number of common stocks in issue.

The profit attributable to equity shareholders is the profit after tax and after exceptional and extraordinary items, and after deducting dividends to preferred stockholders and, in the case of the accounts of a group of companies, after deducting dividends to minority shareholders.

The number of common stocks in issue is a weighted average number of shares to allow for any new share issues during the year.

$$\text{Earnings per share} = \frac{\text{Profit attributable to equity}}{\text{Number of equity shares}}$$

Earnings per share is a measure of the return on profits or, for each equity share in a period, normally one year that makes no distinction between the amount paid in dividends and the amount retained in the business.

Volatility of EPS

A problem with EPS as a measurement of equity returns is that earnings can fluctuate substantially from one year to the next. Dividends, by contrast, usually are more stable. Companies can maintain a dividend, even when profits have fallen, by reducing the dividend cover.

A reason for the volatility of EPS is that total earnings are calculated after the deduction of exceptional items from profits. Accounting regulations mean that companies often will report quite substantial exceptional items in their annual profits, but these items should be non-recurring. The underlying profits might be stable, or on an upward trend, but significant fluctuations can be caused by one-off items.

Many companies report in their annual accounts at least two figures for earnings per share, EPS measured by the official definition, and EPS measured according to a different definition of earnings, that the company considers gives a better assessment of the underlying profitability of the company's operations.

EPS and P/E Ratios
Earnings per share is still a widely used measure of share performance because it can be related to the value of the share. A price/earnings ratio, or P/E ratio, is simply the ratio of the current price of a share to the EPS. For example, if a share price is $10 and earnings per share is $1, the P/E ratio will be 10.0, indicating that the current share price is valued on a multiple of ten times the company's annual profits.

P/E ratios are used for comparisons of share values in different companies.

Risk and Return

Equity investments are high-risk and returns during a period could be much less than expected, particularly when profits fall or fail to increase at the forecast rate. Equally, returns can be higher than expected when the company performs well. Risk to an equity investor is the possibility, or even the probability, that actual returns will be lower, or higher, than expected. There is a downside to the risk, that returns could be disappointing, and an upside that returns could exceed expectation.

Investors in high-risk securities should expect a higher average annual yield. A higher yield compensates the investor for the risk. Investors will expect a higher average annual return from shares than from investing in risk-free securities.

Risk-free securities are government bonds. In the US, the risk-free rate of return is the yield paid on Treasury bonds with 30 years to maturity (the long bond). In the UK, the risk-free rate of return is the yield currently obtainable on long-dated gilt-edged securities (gilts).

Over time, equity returns should exceed the return on a risk-free investment, but in any particular year or month or week, etc., equity returns could fall below risk-free returns. Stock markets monitor equity returns and returns on government bonds, particularly the difference in the size of returns on each type of investment.

The Capital Asset Pricing Model

Equity shares in general are more high-risk investments than government bonds that are risk-free securities. In addition, the variations in returns on equity, and therefore the risk to shareholders, differs between individual companies. Some companies are more high-risk investments than others, with more volatile returns. For example, if average stock market returns go down by 2%, it might be expected that returns on a high-risk share will go down by more, perhaps by 3%. On the other hand, if the average market returns went up by 2%, the returns on the same high-risk share would be expected to go up by 3%. Greater risk means greater volatility in returns, with the possibility of very high returns compared to the market average, but also the risk of much greater falls in returns.

The capital asset pricing model is a mathematical model or formula for establishing the expected average returns from individual shares or a portfolio of shares, taking into account the volatility in returns on the share.

The model is based on a comparison of:

- the risk-free yield on investment
- the average market yield, i.e. the average yield from the equity market as a whole. This is usually higher than the risk-free yield
- the expected yield on an individual share or a portfolio of shares. This could be higher or lower than the average market yield, depending on the comparative risk.

The size of the yield from investing in the shares of an individual company depends on various factors that can be categorized into two groups:

- factors that are specific or special to the company, e.g. the quality of its management. These factors give rise to specific or unsystematic risk
- factors that affect all firms in the economy to a greater or lesser extent, and not just the individual company. These factors give rise to market risk or systematic risk.

The yield on a share depends on a mixture of factors that are specific to the company and factors that affect the economy and the market as a whole. An investor can overcome the problems of specific risk (unsystematic risk) by diversifying investments, and holding a well-balanced portfolio of shares (an efficient portfolio). Some shares in any period will perform better than expected, due to specific factors, and others will perform worse. In an efficient portfolio, the good performing shares and the bad performing shares will balance out.

Market risk (systematic risk) cannot be eliminated by diversification of investments. When the market as a whole improves, individual shares also should yield bigger returns. When the market performs badly, most individual shares also will perform badly.

The CAPM is used to establish the systematic risk for shares in individual companies, and the return that an investor with an efficient portfolio of investments should expect to receive from his/her shares. This expected yield, ignoring specific risk factors, should determine the share's market price.

Beta Factors

The return from investing in shares should be higher than the risk-free yield. The market return, the average return from the stock market as a whole, can be expressed as a risk-free yield plus an excess return, to compensate investors for the higher risk.

Market return	=	Risk-free return	+	Excess return
R_m	=	R_f	+	$(R_m - R_f)$

where

R_m is the average stock market return, and
R_f is the risk-free rate of return.

Through statistical analysis, the excess returns from shares on individual companies, excluding specific or unsystematic risk factors, over the risk-free rate of return, can be measured. The excess return over the risk-free rate for an individual stock could be higher or lower than the excess return for the market as a whole by a factor ß.

CAPM Formula

The CAPM formula for the expected return from individual shares can be stated as

$$R_s = R_f + ß\,(R_m - R_f)$$

Where

- R_s is the expected return from the share, ignoring specific risk factors
- R_f is the risk-free rate of return
- R_m is the average stock market return
- ß is the beta factor for the individual share, measured by a statistical analysis of historical (actual) returns

When ß = 1, the expected return is the same as the average market return. The beta factor for the stock market as a whole is 1.

When ß = 0, the expected return is the risk-free yield. The beta factor of risk-free securities is 0.

When a share's beta factor is between 0 and 1, its specific (systematic) risk is lower than for the stock market as a whole. When average market returns rise or fall, returns from the share should rise or fall by a lower amount. Low beta factors are associated with defensive stocks.

When a share's beta factor is greater than 1, its specific risk is greater than for the stock market as a whole. When average market returns rise or fall, returns from the share should rise or fall by a larger amount. High beta factors are associated with cyclical stocks.

Example

Shares of Tango Inc. have a beta factor of 1.2. The risk-free rate of return is 4% and the average stock market return is 7%.

An investor with an efficient portfolio of shares will expect the yield from Tango Inc. shares to be:

$$R_s = 4\% + 1.2\,(7 - 4)\% = 7.6\%$$

If the average market return rises to 9%, and the risk-free yield remains 4%, the expected yield on Tango's shares will rise to:

$$R_s = 4\% + 1.2\,(9 - 4)\% = 10.0\%$$

A 2% increase in the average market return, from 7% to 9%, results in an increase of 2.4% (1.2 x 2%) in the expected return on Tango shares, from 7.6% to 10.0%.

Uses of Beta Factors

One use of beta factors and the capital asset pricing model is to assess the likely change in returns on individual company shares, or in returns on investment portfolios, given a change in stock market returns generally.

A second use of beta factors is as a method of establishing the cost of equity in an individual company. This is the return on equity capital that the individual company will be required to achieve to meet the expectations of its shareholders.

EVA® and MVA

Economic Value Added

Economic Value Added (EVA®) is a concept developed by the firm

Stern Stewart as a method of measuring a firm's financial performance. In particular, it looks at whether the company has been creating shareholder value from its investments. Value is created when a company earns a return on its capital in excess of the returns required by its investors. However, companies may invest in projects that destroy value rather than create it.

EVA® attempts to measure economic profits from a company's activities, rather than accounting profits. Stern Stewart have developed techniques for measuring economic profit from accounting profit. Significantly, EVA® is calculated after deducting a cost for equity as well as the interest cost of debt.

EVA® = Economic capital x [operating return on capital – Cost of all capital, equity as well as debt]

Market Value Added

Market value added (MVA) is a measurement of performance derived from the concepts underlying economic value added. It provides a cumulative measure of a company's performance over time. Whereas EVA® measures the performance of a company within one period of time, MVA considers the effect on the market value of the company. Because the market value of a company's shares depends on investor expectations of *future* performance, MVA is forward-looking, and considers the market's perception of the future effects of the company's current investments and business strategies.

Conceptually, MVA is the difference between the current market value of the company and the sum of all the funds that have been invested in the company over its life.

MVA = Total market value minus Invested capital (or economic book value of assets)

There are techniques for measuring invested capital from the accounts of a company by making various adjustments to the accounts values.

If investors believe that the current strategies of the company are sound,

MVA will rise. The value of expected returns will increase by more than the economic cost of new investments. On the other hand, if investors are not convinced by the company's strategy, market value will not rise by as much as the cost of new investments, and MVA will fall.

A number of companies use economic value added and market value added to measure their performance, and the performance of operating divisions within their groups.

3

Share Values

Share prices in the equities markets are determined by supply and demand. The supply comes from companies issuing new shares and investors wishing to sell shares they hold. Demand comes from buyers who are looking for a suitable return from their investment. Expected returns, measured by dividends and share price growth or by profits are therefore an important factor in the market's current valuation of shares.

Liquidity and Share Prices

A liquid market in shares is one in which the shares can be bought or sold readily at a fair price. Liquidity is characterized by a large volume of turnover in the shares, mainly in relatively small-sized transactions. Very large transactions can alter the share price by a large amount and a market is not properly liquid when this happens.

Shares in smaller public companies usually are much less liquid than shares in large companies. The bulk of small company shares often are held by a limited number of shareholders including directors of the company and institutional shareholders. These are mainly long-term investors, and only a small proportion of the company's shares are in the hands of would-be sellers. Individual buy or sell orders could move the price by a large amount.

A market maker receiving an order from a client for the purchase of shares in an illiquid small company stock could have to approach current shareholders to ask whether any of their shares might be for sale. The market maker also will set a wide spread between its bid rate, the price at which it will buy shares in the company, and its offer rate, the price at which it will sell for shares in small companies. This acts as a further disincentive for investors to buy and sell the shares regularly.

How are Share Prices Determined?

Share prices can fluctuate continually in response to buy and sell orders. Prices in most liquid stocks rise or fall each day, usually by fairly small amounts. However, there are differing views about the underlying factors that determine a share's market price and movements in the market price. Two broad approaches to share price analysis are:

- technical analysis, and
- fundamental analysis.

The broad differences between these two methods are set out in the table below.

Technical analysis	Fundamental analysis
The share price in the past and the present provides clues about probable future movements in the share price.	A company's shares have an intrinsic value, based on expected future returns to shareholders.
If the price movements of a company's shares are charted on a graph, certain identifiable patterns become evident.	An assessment of expected future returns should be based on a study of the company, its industry and its markets.
Future price trends can be predicted from these patterns. These can suggest whether and when investors should buy or sell the shares.	This study of the company should concentrate on the strengths or weaknesses of the company, both internal strengths and strengths relative to other companies. The analysis of a company and assessment of expected future returns should indicate when a share seems overvalued, therefore sell, or undervalued, therefore buy.

Technical Analysis

There are three basic systems of technical analysis:

- a relative strengths approach
- Hatch system
- Chartism.

Relative Strengths Approach

The relative strengths approach to technical analysis is based on the assumption that if a share or industrial sector starts to outperform the market in terms of price, it will continue to do so, at least in the short term.

Information about the share's relative strength takes time to filter through the market to all investors. The share price trend gathers momentum, and the price eventually will rise above what the share is worth, before falling back.

Hatch System

The Hatch system is based on filter rules for distinguishing between random short-term variations in a share's price and long-term trends and changes in trend. An investor or analyst must decide what percentage movement in the share price is large enough to indicate a change in trend.

Example

An investor is monitoring the price of shares in Alpha. The share price has been fairly stable around 450¢ for several months. The investor decides that a share price change of more than 10% above or below this price would indicate the start of an upward or downward trend in the price.

Analysis

The investor could chart the movement of Alpha's share price. If the price rises above 495¢ (110% of 450¢), the investor could decide to buy the shares, expecting the price to rise still further.

Chartism

Chartism is the most extreme and scientific form of technical analysis. It is based on the belief that share price patterns that have occurred in the past will be repeated in the future. Trends can be identified, despite short-term random price movements. The techniques for chartist analysis vary. One method is to construct line charts. The price of the share is plotted on a graph at regular intervals, typically daily or weekly, over a period of several months. The points are joined up to form a line.

Trends can be analyzed from a graph, and techniques have been developed for distinguishing between major long-term trends, short-term secondary trends and daily variations (tertiary trends). Significant patterns indicating major trends can be identified, and investors can buy or sell the shares with an expectation of how the trend will continue.

Significant Patterns and Trend Lines

Significant patterns include:

- a support level
- a resistance level
- a trend line with an upper and lower limit.

A support level is a price below which the share price does not fall. The price could rise above this level, but fall back again. If the price falls below the support level, however, a further fall should be expected.

A resistance level is a price above which the share price does not seem to rise. Whenever the price rises to this level, it falls back again. Once a resistance level is breached, however, chartists would expect the price to rise still further.

A trend line, with an upper and lower level, can indicate the general direction in which the share price is moving. Short-term minor rallies and falls will occur within the channel between the upper and lower limits. When the share price breaks out above or below these limits, chartists would predict that the trend has changed.

Support Level

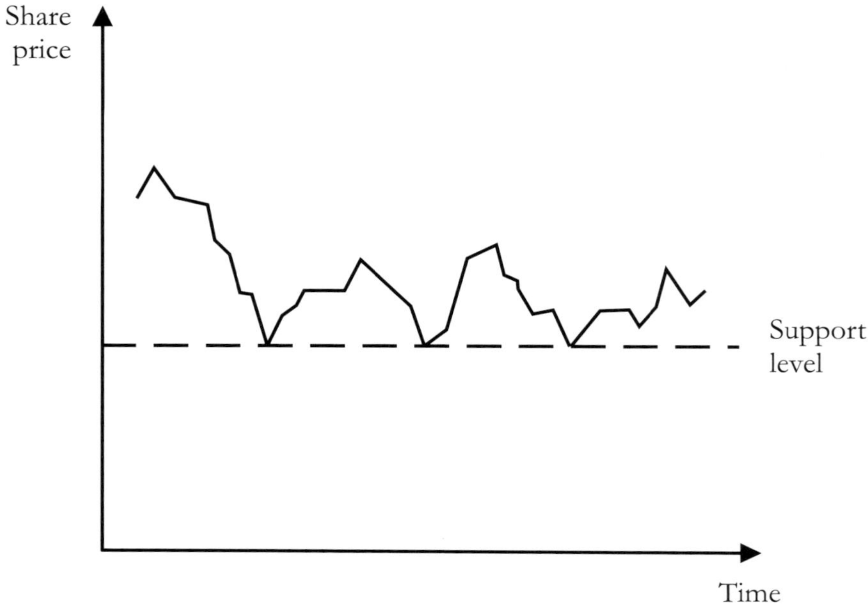

Resistance Level

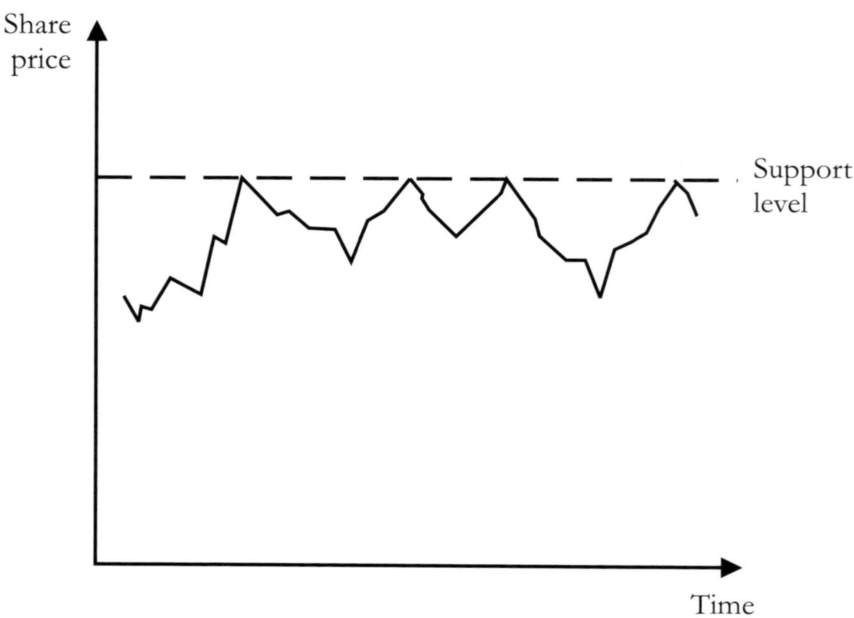

Trend Line

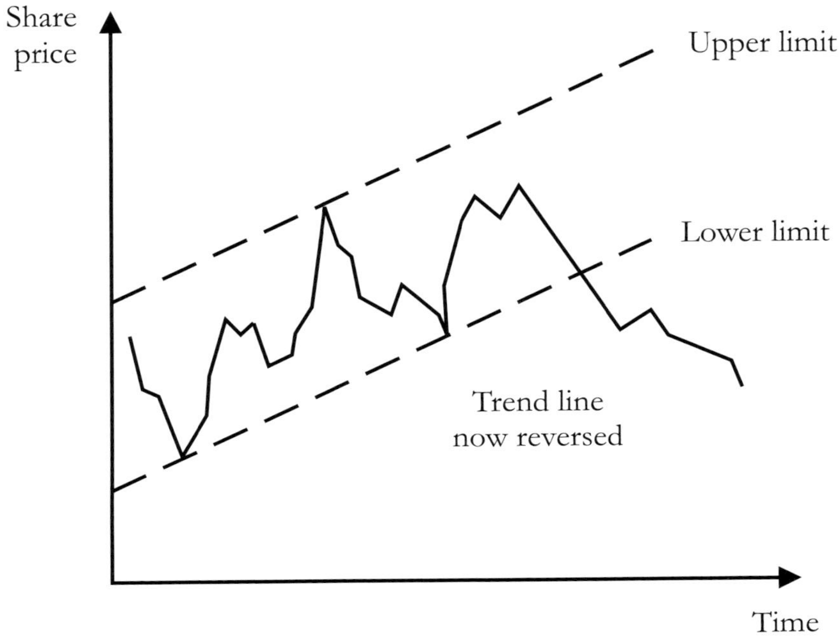

Moving Averages

Moving averages of the share price can be used to monitor a trend in price movements. If share prices are on a rising trend, the average price for the past 20 days should be higher than the average for the past 60 days, and the average price for the past 60 days should be higher than the average for the past year – 240 market days. If the trend changes, the moving averages must at some time cross over, and the average price over a long term will be higher than the average price over a short term.

Moving averages and trends

Upward trend: 20-day average*	> 60-day average	< 240-day average
Downward trend: 20-day average	< 60-day average	> 240-day average

* Average = moving average of the daily share price over a given number of days

Reversal Patterns

Reversals in share price trends also can be identified in several reversal patterns. These include:

- the head-and-shoulders pattern
- the inverted saucer
- the double top.

Head and Shoulders

The head-and-shoulders pattern takes its name from the general shape of the share-price graph. The share-price rises to a certain level, the left shoulder, falls to the neck line and rises again to a peak, the head. This is the highest price that the share will reach. The price then falls back to the neck line and rises again to the right shoulder, to be followed by a large price fall. When the price falls below the neckline, chartists would advise investors to sell the shares quickly.

Head and Shoulders

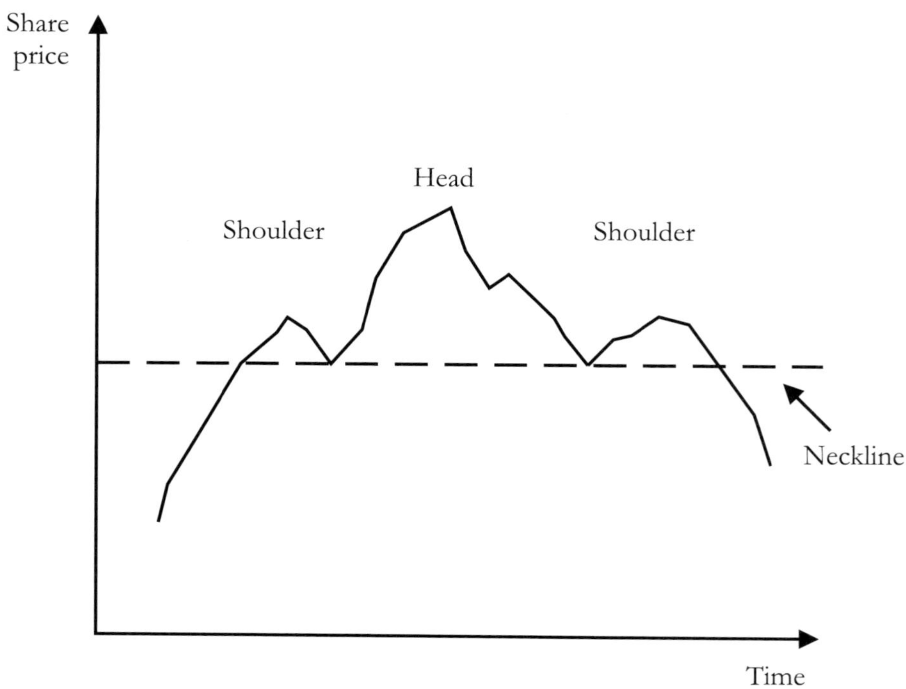

Inverted Saucer

The inverted-saucer pattern of share-price reversal also derives its name from the shape of the graph. The share-price rises gradually to a peak and begins to fall. When the fall is more than a certain amount – below the right shoulder – a continuing fall in price is indicated. Investors would be encouraged to sell the shares.

Inverted Saucer

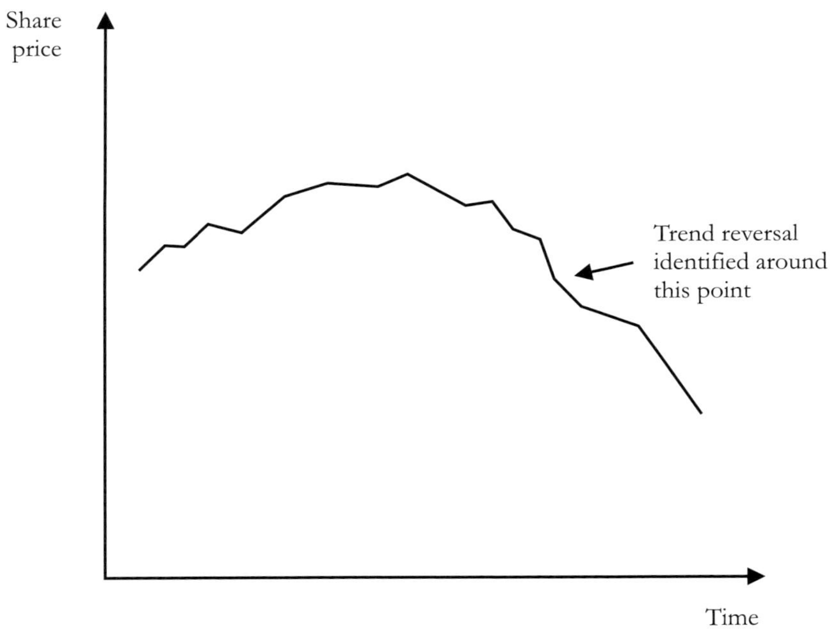

Double Top

A double top is a pattern in which the share price makes two attempts to breach a resistance level. Having failed to do so, a fall in price by more than a certain amount would suggest a reversal in the trend and an even larger fall in price in the future.

Double Top

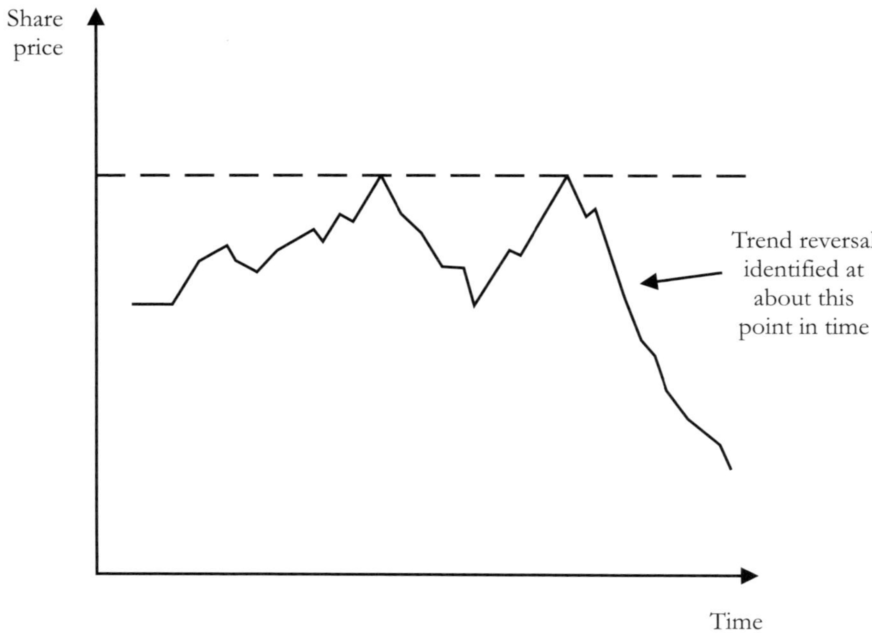

Fundamental Analysis

Fundamental analysis is an approach to share-price evaluation that tries to establish an intrinsic value or true worth for the shares of each company, based on the company's earnings prospects and other factors affecting growth or decline.

Factors taken into consideration include:

Overall economic activity	Factors specific to the industry or sector	Factors specific to the company
Swings in the business cycle	Business cycles in the industry	Expected future profits and dividends
Monetary changes (rate of inflation, changes in interest and currency rates)	Industry structure Competition Costs Labour relations	Quality of management Internal strengths; marketing, research and development, etc.
Fiscal changes	Completion times	
Unemployment level	Barriers to entry Regulation	

Unlike chartists, however, analysts of fundamental share value would not claim to be able to predict short-term variations in the price of a share, only long-term trends.

Dividend Valuation Model

Fundamental theory states that the intrinsic value of a share is the value of all expected future dividends that will be paid to the shareholder. The value is obtained by discounting the expected future dividends at the rate of return required by the shareholders.

When the dividend per share is expected to be a constant amount every year, with no prospects of growth, the intrinsic value of a share can be expressed by the formula:

$$V = \frac{d}{r}$$

where

V is the intrinsic value of the share
d is the annual dividend in price, and

r is the rate of return required by shareholders, expressed as a proportion, e.g. 10% = 0.10.

This formula is slightly simplified because it assumes an annual dividend payment, the next being due in one year's time. Adjustments can be made to the formula, however, to allow for six-monthly or quarterly dividends, and for dividends that are due within the next few weeks or months.

Example

Beta, a public company, is expected to pay an unchanged annual dividend of 56¢ per share into the foreseeable future. The return required by equity shareholders in Beta is thought to be 8%.

Analysis

If the next annual dividend is due in about one year, the intrinsic value of Beta's shares is

$$V = \frac{56¢}{0.08} = 700¢ \text{ per share}$$

Dividend Growth Valuation Model

The dividend valuation model can be adjusted to allow for expectations of growth over time in the annual dividend payments. Varying rates of growth over time can be provided for in the model, but it is simpler to assume a constant annual growth rate. When the dividend on a share is expected to grow at a constant percentage, that is a proportional amount every year, the intrinsic value of the share will be:

$$V = \frac{d\,(1 + g)}{(r - g)}$$

Where:

d is the current year's dividend, excluding any growth

g is the expected annual rate of growth in dividend, expressed as a proportion

r is the return expected by shareholders, also expressed as a proportion

Example

Gamma has just paid an annual dividend of 14¢. Dividends are expected to grow by 5% per annum into the foreseeable future. Equity shareholders in Gamma expect an annual return of 9%.

A market maker in the shares of Gamma is quoting prices of 320-335 for the shares. 320¢ is the bid price that the market maker will pay a seller of the shares and 335¢ is the offer price at which the market maker will sell Gamma shares to a buyer.

Analysis

The intrinsic value of the share is:

$$V = \frac{14¢\ (1.05)}{(0.09 - 0.05)} = \frac{14.7¢}{0.04} = 367.5¢ \text{ per share}$$

The share price is worth more than its current quoted market price, and an investor might be advised to buy Gamma's shares.

Return on Equity: Obtaining a Value for r

The dividend valuation models require an estimate of the average annual return expected by shareholders, an estimate of r must be obtained. This could be derived from a Capital Asset Pricing Model analysis of a company's shares.

P/E Ratio Valuation

It is usual to assess the value of a company's shares on the basis of earnings (profits) rather than dividends, using the concept of the price/ earnings ratio (P/E ratio).

As explained in chapter 2, the P/E ratio is simply the ratio of a share's price to the annual earnings per share.

Example
Tango's share price is currently 320¢. The earnings per share last year were 20¢.

Tango's P/E ratio is therefore 16.0 (320 ÷ 20¢).

The P/E ratio can be very useful for comparing share prices of different companies, particularly within the same business sector.

A company's P/E ratio can be a measure of how risky the market considers investing in the company's shares to be. A low P/E ratio indicates a high assessment of risk or poor prospects for profit growth. A high P/E ratio indicates relatively low risk and/or good prospects for growth in profits and dividends.

A company with a P/E ratio that is lower than the sector average could have the potential for a large price increase, provided the market expects its profits to improve in the future. On the other hand, a low P/E ratio also could indicate that the company is in difficulties and has uncertain prospects for recovery.

Example
A company's share price is currently 400¢ and its earnings per share are 40¢. Its P/E ratio of 10 is below the sector average of 14.

Analysis
If the market believes that the company's prospects are improving, and that it will soon report good profits growth, the company's shares could justify a re-rating to the sector average P/E of 14. Consequently the share price should be regarded as undervalued until it reaches 560¢ (14 x 40¢).

If, on the other hand, the market's expectations for the company take a turn for the worse, a lower P/E rating would be appropriate, and the share price should fall.

Drawbacks to P/E Ratio Valuations
There are several difficulties with a P/E ratio basis of share valuation.

Reliable valuations based on P/E ratios depend on reasonable stability in a company's growth rate in earnings per share (EPS). When the EPS is volatile, fluctuating significantly from one year to the next, it is impossible to establish an intrinsic value for the share simply by applying a P/E multiple to the most recent EPS.

EBITDA Multiples

EBITDA stands for earnings before interest, taxation, depreciation and amortization. Depreciation of fixed assets, and amortization of intangible assets such as goodwill, can be very large items of cost for a company, but they are notional costs only. They represent a write-off of capital expenditure that has occurred in the past, and are not a current item of cash expenditure.

Some analysts regard cash profits as more significant than traditional earnings or accounting profits. EBITDA is a basic and approximate measure of cash operating profits (cash profits before interest and taxation).

Share prices can be assessed on an EBITDA multiple rather than on a P/E ratio multiple.

Asset-Based Valuations

Share values depend primarily on expectations of dividends and earnings, and on yields required by equity investors. Stock market analysts occasionally will look at the value a company's assets, and at the net asset value per share. This is the value of the assets of the company financed by equity capital, divided by the number of shares.

$$\text{Net assets per share} = \frac{\text{Total assets - liabilities - preferred stock capital}}{\text{Number of common stocks}}$$

In many companies, net asset value is a very poor guide to the value of a share. In some industries, however, asset values can be more significant because the assets owned by a company have both a high value and a measurable market value of their own. Investment companies are the main example. An investment company owns a large portfolio of investments, in bonds, shares of other companies, and so on, that have a market value of their own. The share price of an investment company therefore should be close to the value of its net assets.

Analysts measure the net asset value (NAV) of investment companies, and compare this with the share price of the company. When the share price is higher than NAV, there is a premium, and when the share price is below NAV there is a discount. The premium or discount of NAV to the share price, as a percentage, is monitored. If there is a discount, particularly a large discount, analysts might question the performance of the company because it would be much cheaper for investors to buy the underlying investments rather than invest in the investment company.

When the assets of any company, a property company for example, could be sold off for an amount close to their balance-sheet value, and the share price of the company is at a large discount to the NAV per share, investors might consider the merits of calling for the liquidation of the company. In the case of conglomerate groups, shareholders might call for a demerger of the company to unlock value and pay shareholders what the assets of the business are properly worth.

How Reliable is Fundamental Analysis?

The purpose of fundamental analysis is to determine the intrinsic value of a share. The actual share price can fluctuate in a random way around the intrinsic value, but in the long run the average actual price and the intrinsic value should be closely comparable.

The main criticism of fundamental analysis is that, given no significant change in shareholders' expectations about dividends and profits, share prices should remain fairly stable, or grow at a fairly steady rate. On occasions, however, there have been sudden large and unexpected increases or falls in share prices.

Some very large falls that have occurred in share prices could not be properly explained by fundamental analysis because the change in price levels did not have any closely identifiable cause. A significant example of this in recent times was the worldwide collapse in share prices led by New York and London, on Black Monday October 19 1987 when share prices fell by about one third. The collapse in prices, while pointing to a serious over-pricing of shares in the months before Black Monday, could not be explained convincingly by fundamental analysis, such as revised expectations about the world's economy or about future prospects for corporate profits.

Summary

Share prices are determined by supply and demand in the market. In the case of liquid stocks, various methods are used to analyze share prices, and identify over-valued or under-valued shares.

Technical analysis is based on the principle that future share-price movements can be anticipated by looking at historical price changes. Fundamental analysis, based on a dividend valuation model or a P/E ratio valuation model, is based on the assumption that share prices fluctuate around an intrinsic value. There are doubts about the validity of fundamental analysis. A basic supposition of fundamental analysis is that the stock markets must be efficient, providing investors with sufficient information to reach a judgment about the fair value of companies' shares.

4

The Equities Markets

The equities markets serve several key functions.

- They are a source of new capital for companies.
- They are a means by which investors can buy into the equity of companies.
- The provide an exit route for equity investors who want to convert their shares into cash. Unlike bondholders, shareholders cannot wait until a redemption date to cash in their investment.
- In countries where public companies are a major part of the national economy, the performance of the stock markets is an indicator of the general state of the economy.

Primary and Secondary Markets

Stock markets fulfill both primary market and secondary market functions.

The primary equity markets are the markets in which companies issue new shares that are sold to investors. The primary markets are the markets for raising capital.

The secondary markets are for trading in shares after issue. They provide a means by which shareholders:

- can liquidate their investment, i.e. sell their shares at a fair price, and
- alter their portfolio of investments by switching out of some shares and into others.

Although companies do not raise capital in the secondary markets, they are nevertheless important for companies. Without an active secondary market, investors will be more reluctant to buy shares in the primary market. Investment banks or securities houses organizing a share issue will have to reassure potential investors that a liquid secondary market will operate in the shares after issue, and will be expected to explain how this will happen. Banks active in the primary market usually will give an undertaking themselves to maintain a secondary market in the shares, by dealing in the shares on their own account if necessary, or acting as a market maker where the market is quote-driven.

Stock Exchanges and Stock Markets

A distinction might be made between a stock exchange and a stock market.

A stock exchange is a formal stock market, whose trading systems, information dissemination systems and administrative systems are used by the intermediaries participating in the dealing activities on the exchange. Companies whose shares are traded on the exchange and intermediaries operating within the exchange must comply with the rules of the exchange.

Traditionally, a stock exchange has a building with a trading floor, on which transactions in shares are made. In most stock exchanges outside the US, trading is no longer conducted on a trading floor, although there is still a central exchange building housing the administrative departments. Trading is carried out by entering orders into a computer system, or by telephone.

A stock market is a more general term for an organized market in which buyers and sellers trade in securities. Stock exchanges operate a stock market, but a stock market does not need a stock exchange. Examples of stock markets without an exchange are Nasdaq, the international equities market and electronic share trading systems. Stock markets must be regulated, otherwise investors would not use them. In addition to government regulation that applies to all stock markets, stock markets that are not also regulated by an exchange authority will have some form of self-regulation.

Trading Methods: Floor Trading, OTC Markets and Electronic Trading

In some stock exchanges, including the New York Stock Exchange, the largest stock market in the world, shares are traded on the trading floor of the exchange. Brokers take orders from clients and transact them by finding another broker wanting to execute the other side of the deal. The NYSE trading system is described in Chapter 6.

An over-the-counter (OTC) stock market, by contrast, does not have an exchange floor. Transactions in shares are made by telephone between dealers and clients. An OTC market can be very small, consisting of just one dealer making a market in the shares of just a few companies. On the other hand, an OTC market can be very large, consisting of many members/dealers and trading in shares of many companies. Share prices can be quoted on a market information system and transmitted electronically to dealers and investors throughout the country and internationally.

Dealing by telephone is still quite common, but is being superseded by computerized trading systems, where buyers and sellers input their orders to an electronic order book, and orders are matched and executed automatically.

Public and Private Markets

A public stock market is a market in which securities and shares can be bought and re-sold by the general investing public. In a private stock market, there are restrictions on the sale of shares to investors, and shares cannot be offered to the public. Typically, shares can be sold only to a limited group of buyers. In the US, the private placement market is one in which companies can issue shares and bonds, but only to qualified institutional buyers, and in the secondary market only qualified investors can buy or sell.

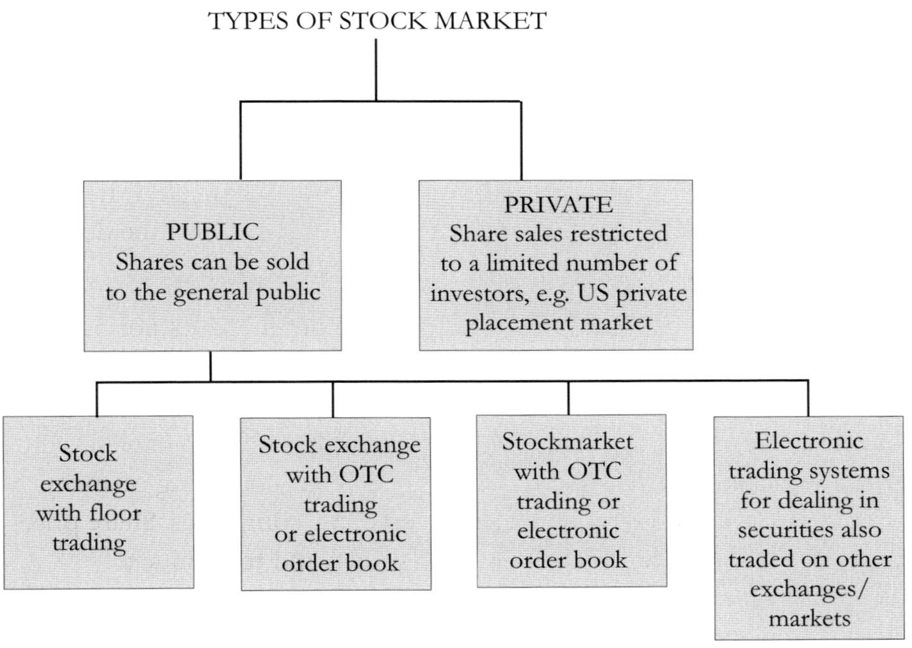

Tiered Markets

Smaller companies can have difficulty issuing shares on a major stock market, for several reasons:

- the high costs of meeting the requirements to obtain a listing
- the high costs and effort of meeting the continuing requirements to retain a stock-exchange listing
- the preference of dealers in a large stock market for trading the

shares of large companies. Dealers could be unwilling to specialize in the shares of smaller companies.

In some countries, there have been attempts to establish special stock markets for smaller and younger companies with mixed success. In the US, Nasdaq has a National Market for shares in the largest companies, and with more exacting listing standards, as well as a market for companies with a small market capitalization, known as small cap companies. In the UK the London Stock Exchange operates a second tier market, the Alternative Investment Market, or AIM. Perhaps the most successful lower-tier market in Europe for high-technology and young companies is the Neuer Markt, part of the German stock market, the Deutsche Börse.

Domestic and International Equity Markets

Most primary and secondary market activity in shares takes place in domestic stock markets. It is simplest to think of a domestic equities market as one in which companies issue shares in their country of residence, for sale primarily to investors in that country. This, however, is an oversimplified view because domestic stock markets are used by foreign companies and foreign investors, as well as domestic companies and investors.

- Some domestic stock markets are used by foreign companies to raise capital by issuing shares and to list their shares for secondary-market trading. For example, UK companies can raise capital in the domestic stock markets in the US, and have their shares traded on a US stock market usually in the form of ADRs.
- Large institutional investors invest in the stock markets of other countries. For example, US and UK pension funds invest heavily in stock markets around the world.

There is also an international equities market, in which major companies can issue shares in more than one country at the same time. The purpose of an international primary issue is to build up a worldwide base of investors, possibly creating a more liquid market in the company's shares. Europe is a major center for the international capital markets, the secondary market is self-regulated by the International Securities Market Association (ISMA), and the primary market by the International Primary Market Association (IPMA), a club of investment banks that operates in the market. Members of IPMA also are members of ISMA, and there is close co-operation between the two bodies.

Issuing Shares in Another Country: Depositary Receipts

A method companies might use to raise equity capital in a foreign stock market is to issue securities in the form of depositary receipts. A depositary receipt is a negotiable security that gives its owner the rights to a quantity of underlying shares.

How are Depositary Receipts Issued?
To raise equity capital in another country by issuing depositary receipts, a company must first issue new shares and place them in the custody of a bank in its own country. A depositary bank in the other country then issues depositary receipts. Each depositary receipt is an entitlement to a specified number of the underlying shares that have been placed on deposit. The depositary receipts are then issued on the foreign market, in the domestic currency of the market. American Depositary Receipts, for example, are issued in the US in dollars.

Whenever the company pays a dividend, the dividend on the new shares is paid to the custodial bank that transfers the money to the depositary bank. The depositary bank converts the dividend into its domestic currency for distribution to the depositary receipt holders.

Depositary Receipts

PRIMARY MARKET ISSUE

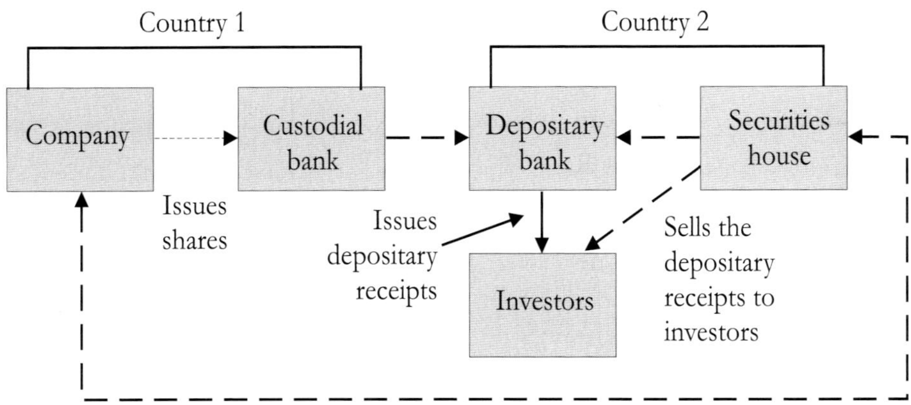

Example
Gamma plc is a large UK-based multinational. It wishes to issue equity capital in the US via the New York Stock Exchange.

Gamma creates ten million new shares, each with a nominal value of £1, and deposits them with a UK bank. A US depositary bank issues two million depositary receipts. Each depositary receipt gives its holder the ownership of five shares in Gamma.

The current share price of Gamma in the UK market is £4 per share and the current exchange rate is £1 = $1.50.

Analysis
An investment bank or securities house that is a member of the New York Stock Exchange will bring the depositary receipts to the market. The issue price is likely to be around $30 (five shares per depositary receipt x £4 per share x $1.50 to £1).

When Gamma pays a dividend in sterling, the depositary bank in the US will receive the payment, and distribute a dollar dividend to the depositary receipt holders.

ADRs, RADRs and GDRs

Although all depositary receipts are issued on the same basic principles, they are called a variety of different names. These include:

- American Depositary Receipts (ADRs)
- Rule 144A American Depositary Receipts (RADRs)
- Global Depositary Receipts (GDRs).

ADRs were the original type of depositary receipt, and are still the most common. This is the name for the depositary receipts issued through a public US stock market such as the New York Stock Exchange or Nasdaq. Most ADR programs are for European companies, although some companies in Australasia, the far east and central and South America also have programs. Depositary banks in the US include the Bank of New York and Morgan Guaranty Trust Company.

When companies have shares traded in ADR form on the New York market, the share price in New York and the share price in the company's domestic stock market could differ. However, it is usual for price movements on the New York market to be in step with the domestic share price. In this way a UK company with an ADR program could find that the share price in the London stock market responds to overnight changes in the New York market.

Rule 144A ADRs (RADRs) are depositary receipts issued in the US private placement market, under the provisions of Rule 144A of the securities code. (Rule 144A is explained in Chapter 6.)

GDRs are depositary receipts issued simultaneously in more than one market. The GDR was first developed in 1990 for the Korean company Samsung. Samsung wished to issue RADRs in the US, but also wanted to make some of the issue available to European investors at the same time. The GDR was a means of making a simultaneous issue in the US and Europe, particularly London. A clearing-house link was established between the Depositary Trust Company in the US and Euroclear and Cedel, now Clearstream, in Europe. This link made it possible for transactions in the GDRs between different countries to be settled by computer entry (global book entry).

Primary Market Issues

A primary market issue involves the issue of new shares by a company for sale to investors. Primary issues occur in any of the following circumstances.

- A company might obtain a domestic stock exchange listing for its shares for the first time. For example, a small company could go public or a nationalized industry could be privatized, through the sale of shares to the general public.
- A company might obtain a listing for its shares on a foreign stock exchange; for example, a non-US company could make a new issue on the New York Stock Exchange.
- A company with shares already traded in a stock market could issue new shares in the market to raise extra capital.

When a private company changes status to a public company and is brought to the market for the first time, existing shareholders, typically founders of the company, make some of their shares available for sale to the investing public. A market is created in existing shares, and the cash raised from the issue goes to the selling shareholders, not to the company. This type of stock market flotation is a secondary distribution of shares, rather than a primary market issue.

An important factor in share issues is often the speed with which a new issue can be made. When issues can be made quickly, a company has greater flexibility in the timing of the issue. An issue then can be timed for when the stock market is buoyant and a good price can be obtained for the shares. The speed of the share issue process depends on the regulations in each market.

- Smaller issues often can be arranged more quickly than large issues.

- There could be a provision within the stock exchange rules for speeding up the issue process. In the US, this can be done by means of shelf registration, a facility now being introduced in the UK.

Methods of Issue

The methods used to issue shares vary between different countries. However, in broad terms, there are three main methods of issue.

- A public offering, in which the shares are offered for sale to the general public.
- Selling all or most of the shares to a targeted group of institutional investors. In the US, there is a separate private placement market. Placing shares with investment institutions is an efficient way of issuing shares in smaller amounts, where the high cost of a public offering is not justified. It is also the method of issuing securities that is used in the international markets.
- In the first instance, offering the new shares for sale to existing shareholders, in proportion to the size of their shareholding. In the UK, the right to buy new shares ahead of outside investors is known as the pre-emption rights of shareholders. Most large new share issues by listed UK companies are rights issues that are described in Chapter 5.

Other methods of raising equity capital include the issue of new shares on the exercise of share options or warrants by their holders.

Listing

Share issues must be approved by the regulatory authorities before they can take place. In the US, issues must be registered with the SEC, and the shares are then accepted by a stock exchange or stock market, where they are listed. A company's shares might have an NYSE listing.

Each country or stock exchange has listing requirements and regulations. Companies must comply with these in order to maintain the listing for the shares.

Registration

In the US, shares cannot be offered for sale to the general public unless they have been registered with the Securities and Exchange Commission (SEC). So with the exception of shares traded in the private placement market for unregistered securities, to obtain a stock-market listing US companies must register the shares before issue.

Documentation for an Issue

Each stock market has its own rules about the documentation that must be made available to potential investors in a new issue. The contents of the offer document or prospectus must include, for example:

- details of the issue, the amount of shares on offer, the issue price, and the reasons for the issue
- information about the past financial performance of the company
- instructions about how to apply for shares.

The rules on the requirements for the documentation for an issue are established by the organization responsible for registration, SEC in the US, or listing, UKLA in the UK.

Sponsoring, Underwriting and Selling an Issue

Sponsor

A share issue by a company is sponsored by one or more member firms of the stock market on which the issue takes place. The sponsoring firm acts as adviser to the issue, and also as the company's representative in its dealings with regulatory and stock market authorities.

The sponsoring investment bank or securities house usually will agree to make a secondary market in the shares after issue, although other firms not involved in the primary issue also can deal in the company's shares, if they wish, and help to create a liquid secondary market.

When an issue of shares is made with the assistance of several securities houses/investment banks, one of them acts as lead manager for the issue. The lead manager is the main adviser to the company. It arranges the underwriting and co-ordinates the efforts of the banks helping to sell the issue to investors.

Underwriters

A company can make sure that all the shares in an issue will be sold by having the issue underwritten. Underwriting is a form of insurance, whereby an institution agrees to take up a specified quantity of the shares in an issue, at the issue price, if there are insufficient other buyers. In return, the institution receives an underwriting commission. The amount of commission is a percentage of the issue value of the shares underwritten, and is payable whether or not the shares have to be taken up.

Example

Delta is planning an issue of ten million shares at a price of 500¢ per share. The full issue has been underwritten and the underwriters' commission is 1.5%.

Analysis

The underwriters will receive $750,000 (1.5% x 10 million x 500¢).

If the issue is successful, the underwriters do not take up any of the shares. If the issue is only partly successful, they must take up a quantity of shares pro rata to the amount they have underwritten. In this example, if there are subscriptions for just five million of the shares, 50% of the amount on offer, the underwriters must take up one half of their underwriting quota at 500¢ per share.

Sub-Underwriters

A lead underwriter, typically the sponsoring organization for the issue, might agree to underwrite the entire issue. Usually it will offload some of the risk by arranging for other organizations to underwrite a part of its quota for a smaller commission. This is called sub-underwriting. For example, if a company is planning a new issue, the entire issue might be underwritten by its sponsoring investment bank for a commission of 1.5%. The bank might obtain sub-underwriters, each to take up a quantity of the shares for a commission of 1.25% for example.

Who are Underwriters?

Underwriters can be securities houses and investment banks, and sub-underwriters could be securities houses, investment banks and institutional investors.

Example

An insurance company already holds 5% of the shares of Theta. The company is planning an issue of 20 million shares at 400¢ per share. The insurance company agrees to act as a sub-underwriter for one million shares, for a commission of 1.5%.

Analysis

The insurance company will receive a commission of $60,000 (1.5% x 1 million x 400¢).

When the issue takes place, it can choose one of the following courses of action.

- It could subscribe for some of the new shares at 400¢, and take a further quantity if the issue is unsuccessful and the underwriters are required to take up shares.
- It could subscribe for none of the shares, but take up a quantity as underwriter if the issue is unsuccessful.

When to Underwrite?

The decision about whether or not to have an issue underwritten depends on how successful the company and its advisers thinks the issue will be. As a general rule there are greater risks with larger issues. It is more usual therefore to underwrite public offerings and rights issues. Issues of securities in the international markets also are underwritten. However, a small placing of shares with targeted investment institutions should not require underwriting.

Book-building

Book-building is a method of selling or underwriting an offer of securities that is similar in many ways to a placing. It is used for international equity offerings and for some large share offers in domestic equities markets.

In such circumstances, the investment bank responsible for selling the shares to investors, referred to as the manager of the issue or book-builder, approaches potential investors, typically institutional investors, and tries to interest them in applying for shares. If they are interested, they are asked how much they would be willing to pay for the shares and how many shares they might be willing to apply for at that price. The prices they bid enable the manager for the issue to decide what the price for the issue should be, to be sure that the share issue is taken up in full. The manager is said to be running a book, hence the name book-building.

The book-runner also will underwrite the issue, in case not enough investors can be found at an acceptable price for the shares.

Book-building is used for international equity offerings and book-runners have good contacts with investors in other countries. By using the book-building process for a domestic share offering, a company might succeed in gaining better exposure, as well as selling its shares to a broad international investor base.

The book-runner asks potential investors what price they would be willing to pay for the shares. Consequently there is a possibility, particularly when the issue is likely to prove popular and to be over-subscribed, that the issue price for the shares will be higher if book-building is used than if the traditional method of deciding the share price by judgment were to be used.

Gray Market

When a new issue has been announced, but before the issue price for the shares has been announced, a gray market in the shares might be operated by dealers. In a gray market, investors buy and sell shares that have not been issued so the sellers cannot deliver them to the buyers, settlement therefore is deferred until after the issue has taken place.

Dealers in the gray market might hope to make a profit by buying or selling the shares at a more favorable price than they will get when the issue has taken place. An advantage of the gray market for the issuer and its advisers is that prices in the gray market will give them a good idea of market sentiment towards the issue, and might help them to decide on the issue price.

Success of an Issue

A successful share issue is one in which there is oversubscribed demand for the shares on offer, so that:

- the company is able to raise the capital it wants, and
- there is likely to be strong demand in the secondary market after the issue, and the share price is likely to rise.

On the other hand, a company will want to avoid very heavy over-subscription for the issue. Over-subscription would suggest that the issue price is too low, and that the company could either have raised more capital, or issued fewer shares at a higher price.

When an issue is thought to be heavily under-priced, a number of investors might try to stag the issue. Stagging is a term used in the UK to mean subscribing for as many shares as possible, with the intention of reselling them quickly after the issue at a profit.

Issues that fail generally do so because of unexpected events between the time the issue is announced and the time it takes place. If the company's share price falls, for example, the issue could fail because it is overpriced.

Issue Costs

The typical costs of a share issue include:

- fees of the sponsor or lead manager for the issue
- underwriting commissions, when the issue is underwritten
- selling commissions to any banks that assist with the sale
- a listing fee to the listing authority and/or a fee to the stock exchange for admission of the shares to trading
- fees of solicitors and auditors
- costs of producing, printing and distributing the offer document
- costs of advertising the issue.

Although total costs are lower for small issues, they can be a higher percentage amount of the total funds raised.

The Secondary Equities Markets

A secondary market is for trading in shares after issue. For a secondary market to function efficiently, there has to be:

- a liquid market and low transaction costs
- an effective system for arranging buy and sell transactions through dealers
- a share-price information system
- an efficient system for the clearing and settlement of transactions.

Different stock markets can be compared on their relative strengths and weaknesses in these areas.

Liquidity

Liquidity varies considerably between stock markets. Investors are more likely to be attracted to liquid markets, where they can be confident of finding willing buyers or sellers whenever they wish to make a share transaction. The most liquid markets generally are the largest, such as the New York Stock Exchange, Nasdaq, Tokyo and London.

Some individual stocks are more liquid than others. Liquid stocks most often are those of large companies, and secondary-market turnover is high. In the case of some small companies, most of the shares are held by a relatively small number of long-term investors, and turnover in the shares is low.

A secondary market is said to have internal efficiency when transaction costs are low, that is transaction costs as a percentage of the value of the transaction. Low transaction costs should help to improve market liquidity.

Dealers and Dealing Systems

A secondary market depends on its network of brokers and dealers. Firms of brokers provide a link between individual investors and dealers or other investors in the market, executing orders on their clients' behalf. To operate effectively, a stock market needs firms that are willing to deal in shares, continually buying and selling the shares of particular companies, and making their profit from the difference between their buying and selling prices. The functions of a dealer or market maker are to maintain a market in shares, and to balance demand and supply through the share price.

There are two types of market dealing:

- an order-driven market, and
- a quote-driven market.

In an order-driven market, sell orders and buy orders come to the market, where they are matched and executed. Current trading information is made available to investors and their brokers so that they will have some idea of the price at which they might be able to buy or sell shares, and they submit their orders accordingly. Some firms act in the market as brokers for clients, but also deal on their own account, to make a profit from buying and selling the shares. These firms are called broker dealers in the shares of the companies in which they specialize. A broker dealer adds liquidity to an order-driven market by balancing supply and demand from other investors, and buying or selling when other buyers or sellers are not available.

Examples of order-driven stock markets are:

- the trading system of the New York Stock Exchange
- electronic systems that use an electronic order book, such as the system for trading shares of the largest companies on the London Stock Exchange (SETS), and the NSC trading system of the Paris Bourse/Euronext.

In a quote-driven market, some firms undertake to make a market in the shares of particular companies by quoting continuous bid and offer prices in the shares. A bid price is the price at which a market maker will buy the shares and an offer price or ask price is the price at which it will sell the shares. A market maker will expect to profit from buying and selling shares at the spread between its bid and offer prices, although it will raise or lower its prices according to supply and demand in the market, or changes in market conditions. When there are several market makers in the shares of the same company, they will compete with each other for the business of investors. An investor wishing to buy or sell shares will choose the market maker quoting the most favorable price – highest bid or lowest offer – and the stock market rules normally require the market maker to deal at its quoted prices.

Examples of quote-driven trading systems are:

- Nasdaq's market maker dealing
- Trading in shares of most companies on the London Stock Exchange below the largest-sized companies (SEAQ).

Pricing

The efficiency of secondary-market trading depends on investors having ready access to current price information. All the major stock markets ensure that this information is fed instantly to users of the market.

A stock market is said to be externally efficient when prices quoted by dealers respond rapidly to new information about company prospects.

Clearing and Settlement

At one time the focus of new technology in the stock markets was on the development of electronic price dissemination systems and electronic trading systems. These are still important, but in addition there have been considerable changes in the systems for clearing and settlement of transactions.

A transaction made between a buyer and seller has to be carried out once it has been agreed. For example, suppose that a broker buys some shares from a dealer on behalf of a client. The transaction, having been made, must be settled by the seller delivering the securities to the buyer, and the buyer paying for them. Between the trade when the agreement to buy and sell is made, and eventual settlement, the transaction must be cleared. Clearing can be defined as carrying out the procedures to make settlement possible at the required time.

At one time, the clearing of transactions involved a large amount of paperwork. The buyer and seller of shares would each write down the details of the transaction on a trade ticket. Back-office staff in the buyer's and seller's organizations would then copy the details and confirm the details with each other, to make sure that each side agrees on what has been bought and sold. Instructions for payment would then be sent to a bank by the buyer. The seller would make arrangements for the share certificate to be made available for delivery to the buyer at settlement.

This process was burdensome and time-consuming. The New York Stock Exchange that handled a huge number of transactions daily, had a paperwork crisis in the 1970s when the exchange had to close regularly to allow back-office staff to catch up with the backlog of clearing and settlement work. The Depository Trust Company and the National Securities Clearing Corporation were set up in the 1970s with the objective of dealing with the problem.

In some markets, clearing and settlement still involves paper work, but in many stock markets most of the operations have been largely computerized. In particular:

- Central securities depositories are able to hold securities on behalf of participants in book-entry form. The securities of each participant are maintained in a computerized stock account, without the need for share certificates.
- Both sides to a transaction confirm the details of the trade by inputting the trade details to an order-processing system operated by the central securities depository. Order details input by each party are matched and confirmed electronically.
- Payment instructions can be sent to the buyer's bank electronically via the central securities depository. The CSD's clearing system also will require the buyer's bank to confirm that the buyer has sufficient credit to make the payment on settlement date.
- At settlement, the shares can be transferred from the buyer's stock account to the seller's stock account at the CSD without any need for a transfer of paper certificates.

A stock market has rules for the settlement cycle, and transactions must be settled on or by a particular time on a settlement date in a system of rolling settlement. The settlement date is a specific number of days after the trade date, i.e. the day when the transaction between buyer and seller was made. When settlement takes place five days after the trade date, this is called T + 5 settlement. The settlement cycle has been reduced in recent years because of the vastly improved efficiency of clearing and settlement systems.

It is now possible to achieve settlement on the same day that the trade is made. Most of the large stock markets have T + 3 settlement, three working days after trade date, including the US stockmarkets and the London Stock Exchange.

Central Counterparty and Novation

Clearing and settlement also have been improved in some markets by the use of a central counterparty for all transactions. A central counterparty is an organization that steps in after a transaction has been made between a buyer and a seller of securities, and becomes the seller to every buyer of securities and the buyer to every seller.

The original transaction between buyer and seller becomes two separate transactions, each with the central counterparty, as soon as the buyer's and seller's trade details have been successfully matched and confirmed.

In the US, the National Securities Clearing Corporation, a part of the Depository Trust and Clearing Corporation (DTCC) acts as the central counterparty on behalf of different stock exchanges in the settlement of all broker-to-broker trades in equities in the US. A similar central counterparty service is provided for the Paris Bourse by Clearnet. In the UK, the London Clearing House began to act as a central counterparty for the London Stock Exchange for share trades made through its SETS electronic order book.

A central counterparty can serve two valuable purposes.

- It guarantees performance of the transaction to every buyer and seller. Instead of having to worry whether the buyer will pay for the securities as promised, a seller of shares can now rely on the exchange for performance. Similarly, instead of worrying whether the seller will deliver the securities at settlement, a buyer can rely on the exchange.
- Many brokers and dealers carry out a very large number of transactions each day, and so settle a large number of transactions daily. Settlement is with the other party to the transaction. When there is a central counterparty, all transactions are settled with just the one other party. This means that instead of settling each transaction individually, it

should be possible to settle all the transactions for one day by means of a single payment, to or from the central counterparty. Settlement of numerous transactions by means of a single payment is called netting.

The use of netting is not yet widespread, but will develop over time. It is used by the National Securities Clearing Corporation in the US for settlements by brokers.

Summary

The stock markets of the world compete for business. For example, the US markets encourage foreign companies to raise capital in the US. The London Stock Exchange trades the shares of a number of foreign companies in competition with their domestic stock exchanges, but is being challenged for supremacy in Europe by both the Deutsche Börse and Euronext, the exchange created by the merger of the Paris, Brussels and Amsterdam exchanges in 2000. Companies and investors can be attracted towards the most efficient and liquid markets for primary issues and secondary-market trading.

US Equities Markets

The equities markets in the US are important sources of capital, not just for US companies but also for a large number of non-US companies. Although US investors purchase shares in markets outside the US, a much larger potential investor base exists for companies that can issue securities in a US market. Non-US companies can raise capital in the US by either:

- issuing registered securities on a recognized stock market, or
- issuing unregistered securities on the private placement market. The Securities and Exchange Commission opened up the private placement market to non-US companies in 1990 by introducing Rule 144A.

With the exception of a number of Canadian companies most non-US companies issue shares in the US in ADR form.

The Securities and Exchange Commission

The SEC is the regulatory body for the US securities industry. It enforces the requirements of the 1933 Securities Act and the 1934 Securities and Exchange Act and from time to time amends the regulations.

Registration of New Public Offerings

After the Wall Street Crash in 1929, the US government introduced several laws to protect investors. One of these, the 1933 Securities Act, requires a detailed registration for any security before it is offered for sale to the public. A condition of registration is the preparation of a prospectus for the issue that must be made available to all potential investors. The prospectus must include information about the nature of the issuer's business and the reasons for the issue, together with detailed financial information about the issuer. Registration is a lengthy, laborious and costly process. However, an issue of shares cannot be offered for sale to the general public in the form of retail investors, as distinct from institutional investors, without being registered. Unless a company is prepared to issue unregistered shares in the private placement market to institutional buyers it must go through the registration process.

Shelf Registration (Rule 415)

To reduce the time required to prepare an issue for public offering, Rule 415 under the Securities Act, was introduced in 1982. This allows an issuer to register and document issues in advance and put them on the shelf for a future offering with only a few details to be added when the issue takes place. This is known as filing a shelf. A shelf registration allows a company to issue shares within just a few hours, taking advantage perhaps of a favorable window of opportunity in the market, for example to issue the shares at a high price.

EDGAR

Electronic (paperless) systems have become essential and inevitable as stock markets have grown in size and activity levels. The administrative task of collecting and processing vast volumes of paper can undermine the ability of an exchange to function efficiently and of regulators to monitor and control the market effectively.

Electronic Data Gathering, Analysis and Retrieval (EDGAR) is a system operated by SEC that allows companies to file information electronically. All electronically filed data can be accessed via databases by the public.

The Main US Stock Markets

There are a number of traditional stock exchanges in the US. The largest of these, and still the largest stock market in the world, is the New York Stock Exchange (NYSE). The second largest in size of the traditional exchanges is the American Stock Exchange (Amex). There are five other traditional exchanges, the Pacific, the Midwest, the Boston, the Philadelphia and the Cincinnati Stock Exchanges. These five exchanges list some stocks exclusively, normally those of smaller local companies, but also have dual listings of other stocks that are also listed on either the NYSE or Amex.

The second largest stock market in the US is the Nasdaq Stock Market. This began operations in 1971 as an automated over-the-counter securities trading system, introduced by the National Association of Securities Dealers. Until its name was changed in 1990 to the Nasdaq Stock Market, it was called the National Association of Securities Dealers Automatic Quotations system.

There are also several electronic trading systems. These allow their participants to trade with each other in stocks through a central electronic order book. Some electronic trading systems also have a link with Nasdaq, and users can trade their securities through Nasdaq if they are unable to find a match within the electronic system itself.

In the US, trading on most of the main stock exchanges is still floor-based. All buy or sell orders are sent to a specialist in the stock who occupies a particular position on the exchange floor. There is a specialist for each individual stock that is listed on the exchange.

Over-the-counter trading (OTC trading) in its original sense, means trading in shares that are not listed on a stock exchange. The meaning of OTC has developed, however, and also means trading that takes place by phone. Nasdaq has described itself as an OTC market for this reason.

Third Market

In the US, when shares are listed on a stock exchange, by no means all trading in the shares goes through the exchange. This is in contrast to London, for example, where most trading in listed shares is still routed through London Stock Exchange dealers.

The term Third Market refers to OTC trading or electronic trading in shares listed on an exchange.

- Dealers who are not members of the exchange can make a market in any listed stock they choose, although they are likely to choose heavily traded shares, for which there is most demand. Their clients are mainly investment institutions.
- Electronic trading systems provide a system for investors to trade directly with each other without the need for an intermediary broker dealer.

The New York Stock Exchange (NYSE)

The New York Stock Exchange (Wall Street) is the world's largest stock market. Trading during normal trading hours is conducted on the trading floor of the exchange, but the trading system is highly automated, and provides immediate dealing services for brokers across the country.

The volume of share trading is huge, and share prices are determined by auction, i.e. by supply and demand of bids and offers coming to the floor of the exchange to be executed. All buy and sell orders in the shares of a particular company come to an assigned location on the floor of the exchange, and all transactions in the shares of the company are executed at that location, between floor brokers or by the market's specialist in the shares.

NYSE Specialists

There are 17 trading posts on the trading floor, each manned by a specialist and a team of specialist's clerks. Every security has a unique trading location at one of these posts, where trading information about the securities are displayed on screens.

The specialist is responsible for maintaining a fair, orderly, and liquid market in a particular group of stocks. They record public orders that come into the exchange and are executed, and execute some orders on behalf of the client. They also buy and sell securities on their own account.

A rule of the exchange is that specialists must execute public orders ahead of their own. If public orders cannot be matched in the auction trading, a specialist has an obligation to provide a continuous market by buying or selling securities on his own account to complete the transaction. Member firms of the exchange may send orders electronically to the specialist through the NYSE Super DOT communication system. The specialist then represents these orders in the trading crowd.

Floor Brokers

There are about 1,500 trading booths around the perimeter of the trading floor where floor brokers take incoming orders, either by phone or electronically, through the Broker Booth Support System. Once a floor broker receives an order, he or she represents the order as an agent in the trading crowd, and executes it on behalf of the client.

How a Transaction is Executed

A buyer sell order originates with an investor who places the order with his or her broker, a member brokerage firm of the NYSE. The investor will maintain an account with the broker, who will check the details of the account to ensure that an investor selling stock has sufficient quantities of the stock for example, before entering the order in its Order Match system. The order is then transmitted electronically to the NYSE, usually electronically but possibly by phone.

On receipt of the order, and depending on its details, the NYSE routes the order either to the booth of a floor broker on the trading floor, or directly to the specialist for that stock.

- If the order is routed to the specialist, the specialist exposes the order in the auction market, and makes the trade at the best available price.
- If the order is sent to a floor broker, the broker takes it to the

area of the trading floor where the stock is traded, competes in the auction with other brokers for the best price and makes the trade.

Once the orders have been executed, a transaction report is sent back to the originating brokerage firm. The brokerage firm updates its account for the client, and sends the client a trade confirmation. If the client is purchasing stocks, he will be required to submit payment. If he is selling stocks, his stock account will be adjusted accordingly.

For stock transactions, there is a three-day settlement cycle, transactions are settled on T + 3. The clearing and settlement system is described below.

Electronic Links to the NYSE

Member firms of the NYSE, located throughout the US, each have an electronic link to the exchange. The NYSE refers to these links as an electronic pathway and the system is called SuperDOT. (Super Designated Order Turnaround.)

The SuperDOT links allow member firms across the US to route orders directly to the trading post of the exchange where the stock is traded, or to a floor broker at the exchange. Orders are then executed and reported back to the member firm's office via the link, typically within 30 seconds. The member firm can then immediately confirm the transaction to its client.

By means of this network, an account executive in a member firm in Los Angeles for example, can transmit an order on behalf of a client to the NYSE, and without any of the firm's own personnel having to take any further action, the transaction can be executed and reported back less than 30 seconds later.

Circuit Breakers

A circuit breaker is an automatic halting of stock market activity whenever trading conditions become volatile. The aim of circuit breakers is to prevent excessive volatility in share prices, and to enhance investor confidence in the system. The need for circuit breakers was recognized after the dramatic collapse in share prices on Black Monday October 19 1987, and was introduced in 1990.

The most routine programed circuit breaker is triggered by a movement, up or down, by more than a specific number of points in the Dow Jones Industrial Average index.

Nasdaq Stock Market

The NASD is the National Association of Securities Dealers, a self-regulatory organization of broker dealers for the securities industry that was first established in 1939. Its members include almost all US broker dealers conducting securities business with the public. The NASD set up the Nasdaq market in 1971, and it has become a stock market with ambitions to be a global market.

In the US, it operates a market for Nasdaq-listed stocks.

- There is a Nasdaq National Market for stocks of the largest companies that requires higher listing standards than for other stocks, and for which there is real-time trade reporting to the market.
- Nasdaq also operates a market in unregistered Rule 144A securities. Rule 144A is described below.
- It also operates an OTC Bulletin Board, giving investors information about, and access to, securities in smaller companies that are not listed on Nasdaq.

Features of Nasdaq

Unlike an exchange with a traditional floor-based trading system, Nasdaq does not have a single specialist for each of its listed stocks. Its trading is based on a quote-driven system of market makers, but with some electronic order-driven trading as well.

A number of market participants trade stocks in each particular listed company, through a world-wide computer network linking buyers and sellers. These market participants in each stock, known as market makers, are responsible for maintaining an orderly and regulated market in the stock.

There are in fact two types of market participant in Nasdaq, creating a market in each stock:

- market makers, and
- electronic communications networks, or ECNs, that bring additional orders into the market.

Market makers are independent dealers that undertake to provide two-way quotations in the prices of the stocks for which they make a market, trading on both sides of the market (buying and selling). They compete with each other for orders by displaying their bid and offer prices. Investors, brokers representing clients, will execute their orders with the market maker quoting the most favorable price.

Market makers are one of four types:

- a retail market maker that has a network of retail brokerage offices serving individual retail investors
- an institutional market maker, specializing in handling large block orders of large institutional investment organizations
- a regional market maker, focusing on companies and/or investors in a particular region of the US
- a wholesale market maker, trading shares with institutional clients and broker dealers who are not registered market makers, and with other types of market maker who may need to acquire stocks to settle their transactions with other investors.

ECNs are private electronic trading systems, and were first incorporated into the Nasdaq market in 1997. To be permitted to trade on Nasdaq, an ECN must be certified with the SEC and registered with Nasdaq. When an order is input to an ECN with a Nasdaq link, it is first routed through the electronic trading system to check for matches. If a match cannot be found, it is posted on Nasdaq an as ECN quote. The order then can be executed in either of two ways:

- on Nasdaq, with another party accepting the quoted price, or
- by matching it electronically with a new order input to the ECN.

Examples of ECNs operating within Nasdaq are Archipelago, Island and Instinet.

Market makers in Nasdaq compete with each other by quoting bid and offer prices in a stock, but can also interact with orders brought to the market by ECNs.

Executing a Trade on Nasdaq

Price and trading information is broadcast to more than 500,000 computer terminals worldwide. The terminals allow equal access to the market and market information for all Nasdaq participants.

An investor may want to execute a market order. This is an order that the investor's broker is required to execute at the best available price on the market, whatever this happens to be. For example, suppose that Jones wants to buy 1,000 shares in ZZZ Corporation, a Nasdaq-listed company. He will call his broker, who will look at the price screen for ZZZ Corporation, identify the best price offered, and execute the order with the market maker (or ECN) at that price.

An investor also may initiate an order on-line through the internet, in which case the investor uses an on-line trading account with an on-line brokerage firm. The order is then executed with a market maker or ECN at the best available price.

An investor might want to place a limit order, rather than a market order. A limit order specifies a maximum price for purchasing the shares, or a minimum price for selling shares. For example, suppose that Jones wants to buy 1,000 shares in ZZZ Corporation, but will not pay more than $15 per share. If the best price available is $15 1/8, the order will not be executed. Under the rules of the market, one of the following must now happen.

- A market maker must change his quoted bid price to 15 1/8, and deal at that price, or transfer the order to an ECN where it can be executed at that price.
- Jones' price of $15 must be displayed as the most favorable bid price in the market so that someone coming to the market to buy shares in ZZZ will see that 1,000 are available at this price.

The rules on displaying unsatisfied limit order prices as the best available price in the market were introduced to Nasdaq in 1997.

Nasdaq International

Nasdaq introduced an international service in 1992, providing a screen-based price-quotation system designed to operate across time zones. This allows trading in Nasdaq securities during the early morning hours of each trading day when the London markets are open. This allows firms to trade in Nasdaq stocks in the US or the UK at any time between the start of trading in London and the close of the US markets.

Private Placement Market and Rule 144A

There are some exceptions to the rules of the 1933 Securities Act requiring shares to be registered before issue. In particular, Section 144 of the Act allows the issue of unregistered securities, and secondary market trading in unregistered securities, in cases where buyers of the securities are investors with capital markets expertise and large financial resources.

The private placement market in the US is the market for securities that have not been registered with the SEC. Unregistered securities can be issued and sold to buyers by means of private placement, i.e. by means of targeted selling of the issue to institutional investors. Secondary market trading can then take place over-the-counter, but only between qualified institutional investors. The securities cannot be traded with the general investing public.

An advantage of the private placement market is that although there is a restriction on potential investors, equity or debt securities can be issued without the difficulties and delays of the registration process.

However, there are drawbacks to an issue in the private placement market. The size of the issue cannot be as large as for a public offering, and institutional buyers might be unwilling to pay as high a price for the shares as they would in a public offering because of the restrictions on resale in the secondary market.

Until 1990 the US private placement market was not accessible to non-US companies. This situation changed with the introduction of Rule 144A.

Rule 144A

In 1990, the regulations regarding the private placement market were modified by the introduction of Rule 144A. The purpose of the rule was to create a bigger and more liquid private placement market by opening it to non-US companies for issuing shares or bonds in the US.

A Rule 144A issue is made as follows.

- A preliminary offer memorandum is prepared for the issue. This is similar to a prospectus, but at this stage the offer price is left blank.
- Underwriters for the issue, known as initial purchasers, market the offer to their institutional buyers in the private placement market, and conduct roadshows with the company's management to publicize the offer.
- The company and the initial purchasers agree on the offer price when they have gauged the response of investors to their publicity and initial approach. This price is put into the final offer memorandum that is then published.
- The initial purchasers buy all the securities at a price below the official offer price, and re-sell them at the offer price.

There are several conditions attached to issues of shares under Rule 144A.

- Shares issued in the private placement market must not be of the same class as shares listed on a US stock exchange, i.e. they cannot be fungible with US-registered shares. Shares can, however, be listed on a foreign stock exchange.
- A seller of shares must take reasonable steps to ensure that the buyer is aware that the shares are not registered. The buyer must be a qualified institutional buyer (Qib). A Qib is an institution, acting for its own account, with more than $100 million invested in securities. For a broker/dealer, the threshold is $10 million.

Non-US companies have made extensive use of the Rule 144A market, issuing debt and equity securities, often in ADR form. The market also may be used by non-US companies for the US tranche of a global offering of a new issue of their securities.

Nasdaq provides a screen-based trading system for institutional investors trading in the Rule 144A private placement market.

Clearing and Settlement

Most transactions in securities are carried out through brokers or by large institutional investors. Most securities transactions between brokers in the US and by large investment institutions, in equities, corporate bonds and municipal bonds, are settled through the Depository Trust and Clearing Corporation (DTCC). Transactions on NYSE and Nasdaq, for example, are settled through DTCC.

DTCC was formed in 1999 by the merger of The Depository Trust Company (DTC) with the National Securities Clearing Corporation (NSCC). These organizations were set up in the 1970s in response to the paperwork crisis facing the US stock markets for the back-office tasks of clearing and settlement of transactions.

The DTCC now offers a range of services including:

- a facility for holding stocks in book-entry form
- electronic post-trade processing of transactions for institutional and broker-to-broker trades
- guaranteed settlement
- cash netting on settlement.

The DTC is a central securities depository where investors hold their securities in book-entry form. Transfers of securities from sellers to buyers are by book entry. The DTC also can handle dividend and interest payments for participants, crediting any dividends or interests payable on book-entry securities to the cash accounts of their owners.

The NSCC processes almost all broker-to-broker trades in the US for transactions in equities and corporate bonds. It acts as a central counterparty for all transactions on the exchanges and stock markets using its services. Every transaction between a buyer and seller becomes two separate transactions, one between the buyer and the NSCC and the other between the seller and the NSCC. The NSCC protects itself against credit risk or default risk by taking cash deposits (margin) from its counterparties to transactions.

Settlement of a Broker-to-Broker Trade

A broker-to-broker trade is settled through the DTCC as follows.

A buyer and a seller each instruct their brokers to execute an order, and their orders are executed on a stock exchange or stock market such as NYSE. The transaction information is transmitted to the NSCC. In the case of a transaction in equities, the trading system of the exchange will match and confirm the orders of the buyer and seller so that the order details transmitted to the NSCC are already locked in. In contrast, with most bond trades, the brokers acting on behalf of the buyer and seller each send their transaction details to the NSCC that does the matching and confirmation.

On T + 1, NSCC issues T contracts for the locked-in trades to the brokers, confirming that the transaction is ready for settlement, and stating the payment payable or receivable on settlement. It also assumes responsibility for settlement by becoming the central counterparty to the transaction for the buyer and the seller. The NSCC sends an instruction to the DTC for the stocks being sold to be moved from the seller's account to the NSCC account, and then from the NSCC's account to the buyer account with the DTC. A money settlement instruction also is issued by the NSCC to the settlement bank of both the buying and selling broker.

On T + 2, the NSCC issues to all brokers a summary of all their transactions that are due for settlement the next day, showing the net payment receivable or payable by that broker for all its settled transactions that day.

On T + 3, settlement takes place. Each broker makes a net payment to the NSCC or receives a payment from the NSCC by the Fedwire same-day electronic funds-transfer system.

Summary

Choosing a US Market to Raise Capital

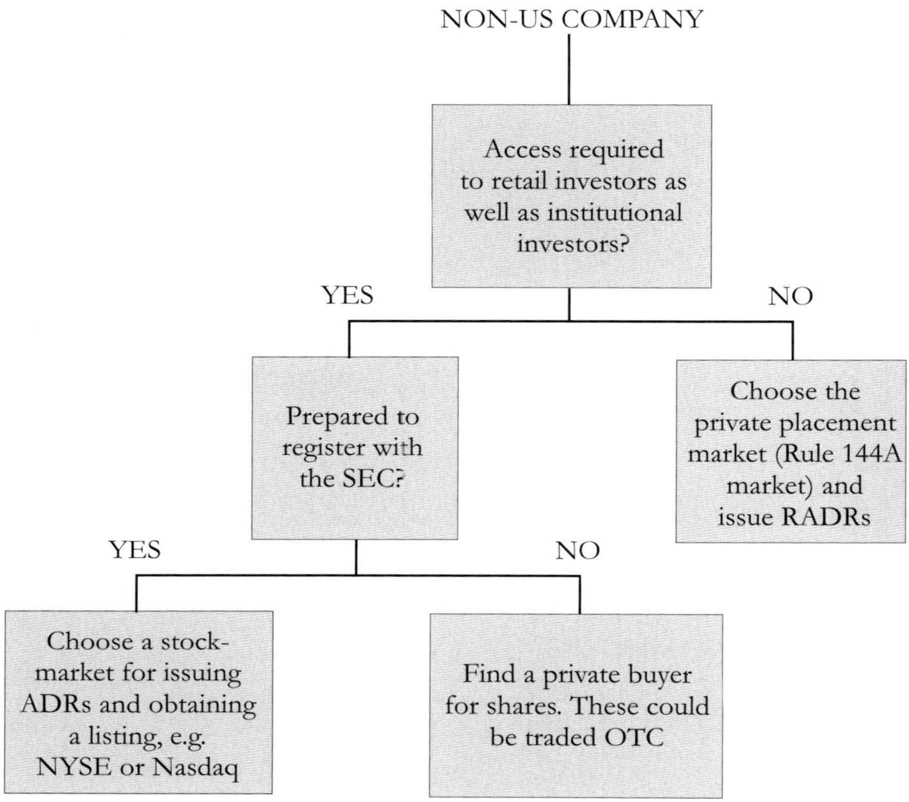

UK Equities Market

The London Stock Exchange is the biggest stock market for equities in Europe. It has two domestic market operations, the main market for large companies and the Alternative Investment Market (AIM) for small companies. The exchange also provides a secondary market for trading in shares and ADRs of various major foreign companies.

The UK Markets' Regulatory Framework

The main UK legislation for the securities industry has been the Financial Services Act 1986 that established a main regulatory authority for the UK financial markets, and is now called the Financial Services Authority or FSA. The Financial Services and Markets Act passed in 2000 extended the regulatory authority and powers of the FSA. All intermediary firms operating in the UK securities markets are subject to regulation by the FSA that is responsible for issuing and enforcing a code of conduct for market participants, as well as the rules governing the admission of shares to listing.

The FSA also recognizes certain exchanges to provide facilities for trading in securities in the UK. These recognized exchanges include the London Stock Exchange.

Primary Market Issues

Most transactions on the London Stock Exchange are secondary-market trades. However, the exchange can be an important source of new equity capital for companies.

There is a requirement under UK company law that when a company already has shares in issue, the existing shareholders should have the first opportunity to buy any new shares that are issued for cash, in proportion to their existing shareholding. These shareholders' rights are called *pre-emption rights*. Shareholders can agree to waive their pre-emption rights. When they do so, the company can issue shares to other investors.

The concept of pre-emption rights is alien to the US, and all share issues are classified as new issues.

The main methods of issuing shares in the UK to raise capital are:

- a rights issue that is an offer of new shares to existing shareholders
- an offer for sale or offer for subscription, in which the shares are offered to the general public
- a placing or placement, or the sale of an issue by book-building.

Rights issues and offers for sale usually are underwritten, so that the company can be guaranteed the money it is trying to raise. For small placings, underwriting should not be necessary, but large issues involving a book-building exercise will be underwritten.

Arranging an Issue: Offer for Sale

It might be useful to look in some detail at the process of making an issue of new shares.

The company appoints a sponsor to arrange the issue and to act as underwriter. An underwriting agreement is drawn up between the company and the sponsor as lead underwriter. The sponsor, as lead underwriter to the issue, then appoints a broker to arrange the sub-underwriting. The broker will contact by telephone institutions that might be willing to act as sub-underwriters, and who will give a provisional commitment to sub-underwrite a quantity of the shares in the offer. This is only a provisional commitment by the institutions at this stage.

The company and its advisers then prepare the prospectus and associated documents. This process is central to the application for admission of the shares to listing that is a requirement for having the shares admitted to trading on the main market of the London Stock Exchange.

In the day or so before impact day, the company makes an application to the London Stock Exchange for admission to trading, the underwriting agreement is finalized, the offer price for the shares is decided, and the company, through its sponsor, prepares its application to the UK Listing Authority for listing.

Impact Day

Investment bankers in London refer to impact day. This is an important day in the calendar for a new issue. It is the day on which the following events occur.

- The final decision is taken to proceed with the issue.
- The price is set officially for the shares, having been provisionally agreed the previous evening by the company and its sponsor.
- The UK Listing Authority gives its final approval to the prospectus for the issue, although it does not yet agree to admit the shares to the Official List. This happens about five days later. The prospectus is the document that the company and its sponsor will use to sell the issue to investors. The prospectus cannot be published until it has been registered with the Registrar of Companies. This normally takes place on impact day.
- A press conference is held and a press release issued, and the offer price is announced to the public.
- The sub-underwriters are sent a sub-underwriting letter that they sign in acknowledgment. A contract thereby is concluded between the issuing house as underwriter and the sub-underwriters.
- Copies of the prospectus are printed in bulk for distribution, to be made available to the general public.

Applications for shares

Publication of the prospectus and advertising the issue begin about two days after impact day. The prospectus constitutes an invitation to the public to apply for the company's shares at the advertised price. Investors wishing to apply for shares fill in the application form and submit it together with a payment cheque to the address indicated – the receiving bank.

The application lists remain open for about a week after impact day. When these applications are being received, the shares will not yet have been admitted to listing.

Admission to listing is granted formally for the shares by the UK Listing Authority about five days after impact day, and the shares also are admitted to trading on the main market by the London Stock Exchange..

Allocation/sale of shares

The applications from investors to subscribe for/purchase shares are processed by the receiving bank. When the offer is over-subscribed some of the applications have to be scaled down. The shares are allocated to successful applicants on the day the application lists are closed. Successful applicants are sent notice that they have been allocated a stated quantity of shares.

Once the receiving bank knows how many shares have been applied for and allotted, it informs the sponsor of the number of shares that have not been applied for and so remain unsold. The issuing house, as lead underwriter for the issue, instructs the broker for the underwriter to allocate the unsold shares to the sub-underwriters in proportion to the number of shares they agreed to sub-underwrite.

The proceeds from the share issue, less commission and fees, are paid to the company.

About a week to 14 days after impact day, the shares are admitted to listing and listing becomes effective. The shares also are admitted to trading on the London Stock Exchange. This means that unconditional dealings in the shares on the stock market can begin.

The share registrar of the company, i.e. the organization appointed to keep the company's register of shareholders updated, prepares the register of shareholders after the allotment/allocation of the shares has taken place.

Stamp duty and SDRT
In the UK, a tax is payable by buyers of shares. The tax is either stamp duty or stamp duty reserve tax, and the rate of tax payable is one half of one per cent (0.5%) of the value of the shares purchased. Stamp duty or SDRT also is payable on purchases of shares in the secondary market, and is very unpopular with investors.

Rights Issues

Rights issues are the most widely used method of raising large amounts of new equity capital in the UK. Shares in a rights issue are offered on a pro-rata basis to existing shareholders, thereby allowing them to maintain their relative percentage shareholding in the company. A one-for-four rights issue, for example, is an offer to existing shareholders of one new share for every four currently held, thereby increasing the number of shares in issue by 25%.

To encourage shareholders to take up their rights, the new shares are offered at a discount to the market price at the time of the announcement of the issue. The size of discount varies, and depends largely on the size of the issue and the company's reasons for wanting the new equity capital. A one for ten rights issue by a successful company that is raising the money to invest for further growth might be offered successfully at a discount of as little as 5% to the market price prior to the rights announcement. In contrast, a one-for-one rescue rights issue by a troubled company seeking funds to shore up its balance sheet might require a discount of up to 40%.

Generally speaking, the maximum proportion of shares that a company can issue without a rights issue being perceived as a rescue rights issue is

33-40%, i.e. a one-for-three or two-for-five rights issue. Beyond this level an issue would be seen as critical to the company's survival rather than an orderly equity capital-raising exercise.

Rights issues depend for their success on the support of the company's major institutional investors. When a rights issue is left largely in the lands of the underwriters, there are two important consequences.

- The share price is likely to remain depressed for a long time because unwanted shares will be hanging over the market.
- Also it will be more difficult to make another rights issue in the future because institutional support will not be so readily forthcoming.

Making a Rights Issue

A company, having established the need for new equity capital, will discuss its requirements with its financial advisers, usually an investment bank or a specialist securities house. The financial adviser usually will act as lead underwriter for the issue; act as sponsor for the issue with the UK Listing Authority; apply to the London Stock Exchange for admission of the shares to trading; and ensure a liquid secondary market in the shares.

The company, assisted by its financial advisers, lawyers and accountants, must then prepare the offer circular. This must include a justification of the need for new equity capital together with the detailed terms and conditions of the offer and an up-to-date explanation of the company's financial position. This preparation and documentation process also includes due diligence by the sponsor for the issue to ensure that the company's financial position is truly represented in the offer circular.

When the offer document is sent to shareholders, the shareholders have until a pre-determined *closing date*

- to take up or exercise the rights, i.e. to buy the new shares at the rights price. Shareholders who do so will maintain their percentage holding in the equity of the company by subscribing for the new shares, or

- to renounce the rights and sell them on the market. Shareholders who do this will have a lower percentage holding of the company's equity after the issue than before the issue

Another option is to do nothing at all. Shareholders are protected from the consequences of their inaction because rights not taken up are sold on a shareholder's behalf by the company. The shareholder gets the difference between the issue price and the market price at which the shares are sold.

Fees usually are about 2% of the value of the issue, for underwriting and selling. In addition, there are the fees for the solicitors and accountants, and for the printing of the offer document. The total cost for a rights issue can be as high as 3.5% to 5% of the total amount raised, depending on the degree of difficulty associated with the issue.

The Offer Price in a Rights Issue

The offer price in a rights issue is lower than the current market price of existing shares at the time the issue is announced. As a general guide, the size of discount might be about 15%-20%. For example, if the market price of its shares was £5 at the time it announces a rights issue, a company might the offer shares at a price of somewhere between £4.00 and £4.40 each. The offer price in a rights issue must be:

- low enough to secure the acceptance of shareholders who are being asked to provide extra funds
- not too low so as to avoid excessive dilution in the earnings per share.

Theoretical Ex-Rights Price

After the announcement of a rights issue, there is a tendency for the share price to fall because the new shares have been issued at below the pre-issue market price. The extent and duration of the fall could depend on the number of shareholders in the company and the size of their holdings.

When a rights issue is announced, all existing shareholders have the right to subscribe for new shares, and so there are rights attached to the existing shares. The shares are described as being cum rights (with rights attached) and are traded cum rights. On the first day of dealings in the newly issued shares, the rights no longer exist and the old shares are now ex rights (without rights attached).

After the issue of shares has taken place, the share price normally will fall because there are now more shares in issue and the new shares have been issued at a discount price. In theory, the new market price will be the consequence of an adjustment to allow for the discount price of the new issue, and a *theoretical ex rights price* can be calculated.

Example
Alpha plc has 100 million ordinary shares in issue. These have a market price on October 1 of £2.63 per share. The company decides to make a rights issue and offers its shareholders the right to subscribe for one new share at £2.10 each for every four shares already held. After the announcement of the issue, the share price falls to £2.55, but just prior to the issue being made, it had recovered to £2.60 per share. This market value just before the issue is known as the *cum rights price.*

Analysis
In theory, the market price will fall after the issue as follows:

	£ million
100 million shares have a cum rights value of (x £2.60)	260.00
25 million new shares will be issued to raise (x £2.10)	52.50
The theoretical value of 125 million shares is	312.50

The theoretical ex-rights price is:

$$\frac{£312.50 \text{ million}}{125 \text{ million}} = £2.50 \text{ per share}$$

The same calculation can be shown as:

	£
Four shares have a cum rights value of (x £2.60)	10.40
One new share will be issued to raise	2.10
The theoretical value of five shares is	12.50

The theoretical value per share is £2.50 (£12.50 ÷ 5 shares)

The actual price after the issue will depend on market conditions, but could be higher or lower than the theoretical price. The theoretical price is useful for judging the market value of the shares, and the mark value of the rights.

Secondary-Market Trading on the London Stock Exchange

The London Stock Exchange has three dealing systems, one for shares in the largest companies, another for companies that are not so large, and a third system for the smallest companies. Two of the systems are described here. One is SETS, an order-driven market, and the other is SEAQ, a quote-driven market.

Role of Broker Dealers

A broker dealer is a participant in the London Stock Exchange that deals with the general public, transacting orders on behalf of clients, but in addition carries out transactions on its own account, buying and selling shares to make a profit on the dealing. A broker dealer can arrange share transactions in any of five ways:

- buy or sell shares though either SETS or through a market maker, on its own account
- buy or sell shares through either SETS or through a market maker, on behalf of a client
- buy or sell shares in a transaction with another broker dealer, on its own account, in a negotiated transaction
- buy or sell shares in a transaction with another broker dealer, on

behalf of a client, in a negotiated transaction
- buy or sell shares in a transaction with a client, on its own account, i.e. with the broker dealer acting as principal.

Trading in Shares of the Largest Companies: SETS

An order-driven trading system is used for trading shares of about 200 companies, including the 100 largest companies that constitute the FTSE 100 stock market index. This system, called SETS, has an electronic order book, that is open from 08.00 to 16.30 each trading day. Member firms of the exchange, brokers and broker dealers, input their bid and offer orders (buy and sell orders) into the system, where they are matched and automatically executed. The orders may be input by brokers on behalf of a client, or by a dealer trading on its own account. Orders that cannot be matched may stay on the order book, visible to all market participants. These orders remain on the order book until they are matched and executed, or until their specified time limit runs out or they are removed by the member firm that entered them in the system.

The order book provides pricing information and a trading mechanism for its users. Orders are executed in strict price and time priority, so that orders are transacted fairly. A representation of the order book for shares in a particular SETS-traded company is shown below.

XYZ	**XYZ plc**	GBX	Close 544		11.50
High 548	Low 542			NMS	10,000
Vol 97,500				Min O.S.	1
Last 547 546 542 545				Max O.S.	200,000
68,200	**Buy**	2,500	22,300	**Sell**	62,000
Time	**Volume**	**Price**	**Price**	**Volume**	**Time**
11.40	2,500	547	548	17,200	11.37
11.15	6,000	546		5,100	11.46
11.32	10,000		549	11,000	11.32
11.20	7,300	545		4,600	11.36
11.33	12,400			9,300	11.41
11.42	5,500		550	4,800	11.01
11.05	8,600	544		10,000	11.07
11.28	12,300				
10.57	3,600	543			

Explanations

This is the order book for shares in XYZ plc that are traded in sterling (GBX). The closing price yesterday was 544p per share. The last trade time so far today was at 11.50 a.m.

The highest price at which the shares have been traded so far today is 548p and the lowest is 542p. Total trading volume so far today has been 97,500 shares. The last four trades in the shares have been at 547, 546, 542 and 545.

The London Stock Exchange assigns every share a normal market size for trading. For XYZ plc, the NMS is 10,000 shares. The minimum order size is one share and the maximum order size is 200,000 shares.

The order book shows orders to buy shares on the left and selling orders on the right. These are limit orders that sit on the order book.

On the buy side, there are buy orders for 68,500 shares waiting for a match, and buy orders for 2,500 shares at the best available bid price. On the sell side, there are sell orders for 62,000 shares in total, and orders for

22,300 shares at the best available offer price. The best prices available on the order book are bid 7, offer 8, referring to the bid price of 547p and the offer price of 548p.

The buy orders waiting to be matched and executed are listed in priority order, with the highest prices at the top, working down. When there is more than one order at the same price, they are prioritized in order of their time of entry to the system that also is shown on the screen.

Similarly, the sell orders waiting to be matched and executed are listed in priority order, with the lowest prices at the top, and orders at higher prices lower down. When there is more than one order at the same price, they are prioritized in order of their time of entry to the system.

Orders are always executed according to their place on the list, in price and then time priority. Orders may be executed in part. In the example above, if a (limit) sell order for 6,000 shares in XYZ at a price of 547p is input to the order book at 11.55 a.m., part of the order will be matched with the buy order for 2,500 shares at this price, leaving 3,500 shares still to be sold at this price. This part of the order will be entered into the order book on the sell side with top priority, because it is now the best offer price available. The top part of the order book would then be as follows.

65,700	**Buy**	16,000	3,500	**Sell**	65,500
Time	Volume	Price	Price	Volume	Time
11.15	6,000	546	547	3,500	11.55
11.32	10,000		548	17,200	11.37
11.20	7,300	545		5,100	11.46
11.33	12,400		549	11,000	11.32
11.42	5,500			4,600	11.36

All orders on the order book are anonymous. Once a trade is executed, the identities of the counterparty is revealed to each party, but not to the market as a whole. Trades executed on the order book are for standard London Stock Exchange settlement, which is T + 3. Each member firm that is a party to a transaction is responsible for submitting details of the transaction to the clearing system, Crest.

Order Types

There are four types of order that can be input to SETS or to any other electronic order book.

- An *at best order*, known in some stock markets as a *market order*, is an order to buy or sell a quantity of shares at the best available price. The order will be matched with those on the order book, in price and time priority, and executed at the best price or prices available. A market order never sits on the order book, but is executed immediately. Any part of the order that cannot be executed immediately is rejected, and does not sit on the order book. At best orders can be very risky, because there is no certainty about the price or prices at which they might be transacted, and it is more prudent to input an order as a different type.
- A *limit order* is an order to buy or sell a quantity of shares at a specific price or better. For example, a member firm of the exchange might input an order to buy 15,000 shares in XYZ plc at a price of 546p or less. If a limit order cannot be executed immediately, it will sit on the order book with other limit orders, in price and time priority. If only part of the order can be executed, the remaining part that has not been executed will sit on the order book.
- A *fill or kill order* must be executed in full immediately, or not at all. It must be entered with a quantity of shares to buy or sell, but it need not specify a minimum price for selling or maximum price for buying. A minimum or maximum price may, however, be specified. If no limit price is specified, the order is matched with as many orders as necessary on the order book in price and time priority, and executed in a number of different transactions, at as many prices as are necessary to execute the order in full. If a fill or kill order cannot be executed immediately in full, it is rejected. It does not sit on the order book.
- An *execute-and-eliminate order* should be executed immediately so far as is possible, for as much as is available in the order book.

> Any portion of the order that cannot be executed is rejected. The member firm entering the order is notified of the part of the order that has been successfully transacted, and also the part that has been rejected without being executed. The part of an execute-and-eliminate order that is not executed does not sit on the order book. Only limit orders sit on the order book.

After the start of the morning session, when the order book must be uncrossed, normal trading in SETS provides for continual automated execution of orders. Limit orders can be input to the system for a short time before the start of normal trading each day, and during this time orders might be entered to buy shares at higher limit prices than orders to sell are input. Consequently the order book might become crossed, bid prices moving above offer prices. The SETS system goes through a ten-minute period each morning, before the start of normal trading, in which limit orders on the order book are transacted and the order book is uncrossed.

Trading in Shares of Other Companies: SEAQ

For trading in shares of companies that are not large enough for trading on SETS, except for the smallest companies, for which a third trading system is used, the London Stock Exchange uses a quote-driven trading system called SEAQ, the Stock Exchange Automated Quotation system.

For a quote-driven system to operate, market firms must be prepared to act as market makers in the shares of particular companies. The role of the market makers is to maintain a secondary market in the securities for which it is registered as a market maker.

For trading on SEAQ (pronounced see-ack), companies must have at least two market makers, although some have many more. Market makers must undertake to provide continual bid and offer prices in the shares to the market. These prices must be firm up to a stated size of transaction, so a market maker must deal at the prices it is currently displaying for any transaction up to this size. Prices for larger transactions are negotiable with the customer.

The SEAQ system is based on competitive price quotations from market makers, and the provision of real-time price information about current prices and recent share transactions to users of the market.

SEAQ has two functions:

- to publish information about share prices and deals, and current price quotations of competing market makers through an on-screen price information service called TOPIC
- to receive reports from London Stock Exchange participants about deals they have transacted.

Market makers must display prices on SEAQ throughout a mandatory quote period each day. During this period, the best execution rule applies.

Executing an Order: SEAQ Shares

Trading in the SEAQ system uses computer technology for displaying prices and reporting transactions, but trading is over-the-counter, by phone.

An investor wishing to buy some shares phones a firm of brokers or broker dealers with instructions that the broker dealer might be a market maker in the shares. The firm of brokers or broker dealers could decide to act as principal in the transaction, but if it chooses to act as agent, it will consult SEAQ by referring to the appropriate price information page on TOPIC. The price screen will indicate which market maker is offering the lowest price in the shares. The broker dealer will then phone the market maker and strike the deal at the quoted price, buying the shares on behalf of the investor. The market maker reports the transaction details to the London Stock Exchange. The market maker may decide, as a result of the transaction, to change its quoted bid and offer prices in the shares.

The best bid prices and the best offer prices being quoted are shown in a touch strip on the TOPIC screen. Prices at which the latest deals have been struck are shown in the line above this touch strip.

Normal Market Size

Market makers must quote prices for a minimum transaction size. This is usually the normal market size (NMS) for the security that is shown on the screen, in thousands, below the company name. The London Stock Exchange has specified 12 levels or bands of NMS, ranging from 500 and 1,000 for illiquid investments, up to 200,000. The stock exchange authorities decide what the NMS for each stock should be.

Market makers also quote their prices firm up to a maximum transaction size that varies according to each market maker. These sizes are shown on the screen, next to each market maker's identity code and quoted prices. The figure 50, for example, would indicate a maximum transaction size of 50,000 shares at the quoted prices and 1L would mean a maximum transaction size of 100,000 shares at the prices quoted.

The NMS of a company's shares can be used to assess their marketability and liquidity by multiplying the NMS by the share price.

For example, suppose that shares in Alpha plc have an NMS of 10,000 and the share price is £2. A normal-sized deal in the share will be £20,000. In contrast, if shares in Beta plc have an NMS of 5,000 and the share price is £6, a normal-sized deal in the share will be £30,000.

NMS and share price are not an altogether reliable indicator of marketability and liquidity, however. For some shares, there are very few trades, and market makers quote a wide spread between bid and offer prices that increases the reluctance of investors to buy and sell the share.

Other important indicators of liquidity are:

- the spread between bid and offer prices. For liquid stocks, this may be about 5p, and
- the volume of trade in the shares.

Information about each of these can be obtained from a TOPIC screen.

SEAQ International
The London Stock Exchange operates a market in the shares of a number of foreign companies. SEAQ International is a screen-based price information system used for these shares. Trading through SEAQ International is similar to trading through SEAQ.

For shares quoted on SEAQ International, the London Stock Exchange is in direct competition for business with the domestic stock exchange(s) on which the shares are listed. For trading in BMW and Allianz shares, for example, London is trading in competition with Frankfurt. An investor wishing to buy or sell BMW shares can do so through London or through Frankfurt.

Clearing and Settlement of Transactions: Crest

Trades executed on the London Stock Exchange are cleared and settled through Crest that settles UK, Irish and a number of international securities in several currencies.

Crest is a central securities depository for the UK that offers its members the facility of holding their securities in dematerialized (book-entry) form as computer entries in a stock account. When a firm or individual holds shares in Crest, there are no share certificates.

Crest also offers its participants settlement of transactions in securities, with payment versus delivery.

Crest Membership
Crest offers membership to both firms and private individuals. All intermediaries and major investment institutions are members. Users have computer links to the Crest system, and communicate with the system through those links. Users must be members of Crest, and a

member who is not a user must communicate with the system through a member who is a user. Such members are called sponsored members. Private individuals who are members of Crest normally are sponsored members, communicating with the system through their bank or stock broker.

Each member of Crest can operate stock book-entry accounts and cash memorandum accounts. A cash memorandum account maintains a record of how much credit the member has with its payment bank. A payment bank is the bank used by the member to settle share transactions, and has a computer link to the Crest system. The bank will provide information to Crest about the member's credit position, and the information is held in the member's cash memorandum account. As part of the clearing and settlement process, the Crest system will check that a member has enough credit in the relevant account to settle the transaction in full.

Crest is not a payments system, and the actual payment for shares by the buyer is made through the banking system. The payment bank simply indicates to Crest how much credit the member has. This might be the actual amount of cash the member has in the account with the bank. When a payment bank indicates how much credit the member has, it must guarantee payments by the member up to that limit.

Settlement of a Transaction in Crest

Two parties who are Crest members execute a share transaction. The parties may be dealing on their own account, or may be a broker acting on behalf of a client. Each party must send electronic instructions about the transaction to Crest as soon as possible after dealing. Crest then matches the instructions so that the transaction is confirmed. Unmatched transactions are given unmatched status until the problem is sorted out by the parties concerned.

Crest then checks that the seller has sufficient stock in the account to deliver at settlement, and that the buyer has adequate cash or credit to make payment. If this is so, the transaction will settle.

At settlement, Crest transfers the stock from the seller's stock account to the buyer's stock account, and the payment bank makes the payment to the seller's designated bank account. The buyer's and seller's cash memorandum accounts may be adjusted.

Other Features of Crest

Crest offers other services to its members.

- It can process dividend payments, automatically arranging for payment of dividends to the legal owners of the shares.
- It collects the stamp duty payable by buyers of shares, and pays this to the government.
- It has links to the DTCC and to other settlement systems in Europe such as Clearstream and Euroclear, to allow the settlement of transactions in foreign securities.

Not all investors are members of Crest. Some who are not members can still hold their shares in Crest by means of nominee accounts. A Crest member will maintain the nominee account on its client's behalf.

Other investors hold their shares in certificate form, and Crest provides a residual settlement service for these investors. Share transactions by these individuals will be carried out for the individual by a broker who will have Crest membership and a Crest stock account. Crest will handle the delivery and processing of the share certificates and stock transfer forms through a special courier service, the Crest Courier and Sorting Service (CCSS).

Central Counterparty

In March 2001, the London Stock Exchange and Crest, together with a clearing and settlement organization, the London Clearing House (LCH), introduced a central counterparty settlement system for trades executed on SETS.

When any trade is executed on SETS, the LCH immediately becomes the counterparty to both the buyer and the seller in a novation process, and there are legal contracts between the buyer and LCH, and between the seller and LCH. As a result, the buyer and the seller never find out who was the actual counterparty to the original trade because their only dealing is with LCH. Providing anonymity to trading on SETS in this way may add to the attractions of the SETS system for broker dealers.

To clear a transaction with the LCH as a counterparty, a firm must be either a Clearing Member of the LCH, or must use the services of a General Clearing Member of the LCH. This is to enable the LCH to operate a system of margin payments that are cash deposits with the LCH to cover the risk of non-performance of settlements by the clearing member.

A SETS transaction will be settled as follows:

- Two firms enter their orders into SETS. They are matched with each other in SETS and executed.
- At the point of execution of the trade, the trade legally becomes two trades, each with the LCH.
- The trade data is transmitted to Crest by the parties where the instructions are matched and the trades confirmed. The buyer and seller each inputs settlement instructions to Crest naming CCP (central counterparty) as the counterparty.
- Crest sends details of the stock and cash positions of the firms, its members, to the LCH that uses the data to calculate how much deposit or margin it will require from each of them. The LCH then transmits these margin requirements to Crest that notifies the firms of the payments they must make.

Settlement of the transactions takes place on settlement date, with stock transferred from the seller's account to the buyer's account, and with the appropriate payments between the LCH and each of the firms.

7

Other Equities Markets

There are many domestic stock markets around the world, varying in size and liquidity, each with its own trading systems and clearing and settlement systems. This chapter gives a brief summary of some of these markets, and the international equities market.

Japan: Tokyo Stock Exchange

At one time during the 1980s, the Tokyo Stock Exchange rivaled the New York Stock Exchange in terms of the market capitalization of its listed securities. Despite the plunge in share prices in Japan in 1989, Tokyo remains one of the largest stock markets in the world, providing listings for both Japanese company stocks and some foreign company stocks, and offering trading in Japanese government bonds.

Shares traded on the exchange are grouped into two sections.

- The first section, or Alpha section, consists of shares in the largest companies. These make up most of the value by market capitalization of listed shares.
- A second section for shares in newly quoted and smaller companies.

Trading in shares is on a board lot system. A board lot is a unit of a given quantity of shares and the size of a board lot varies between companies.

Investors wishing to buy or sell listed securities must go through a firm of authorized securities dealers that will be a member of the exchange.

The Tokyo exchange has undergone significant changes in recent years. Until 1999, most trading in shares was conducted on the floor of the exchange by an auction system called Zaraba. Dealers shouted their bid and offer prices, and made transactions in this competitive auction at the best available price. In 1999 the trading floor was closed, and the auction market, still called Zaraba, transferred to an electronic trading system. The principles of the old auction system remain; that orders should be executed in price and time priority. The market index calculated by the Exchange and disseminated to market users is called TOPIX.

An off-hour trading system for large block orders, using an electronic system called ToSTNeT, also was launched in 1997. An electronic quotations service, Computerized Order Routing and Execution Service (CORES) is available for trading small orders in second section stocks.

All transactions between member firms are guaranteed by the Tokyo Exchange. Its wholly owned subsidiary, the Japanese Securities Clearing Corporation, acts as a central counterparty for all transactions.

Japan has a central securities depository, the Japanese Securities Depository Center or JASDEC. Shares are still represented by share certificates, but these are immobilized and held by JASDEC that maintains electronic stock accounts for its participants, and transfers of stock are made by electronic book entry without the physical certificates being moved.

The Tokyo Stock Exchange (TSE) has a stock account with JASDEC. When a transaction is settled:

- Stocks are transferred by book entry from the seller's account at JASDEC to the TSE's account, and then from the TSE's account to the buyer's account.
- Cash payments are from the buyer to a TSE account at a settling bank or at the Bank of Japan, and payments to the seller are from one of the TSE's accounts.

Settlement is on T + 3. Payments between member firms and the TSE are netted for all transactions settled that day.

Foreign Issuers

Some major non-Japanese companies successfully obtained an equity listing on the Tokyo Stock Exchange and raised new equity capital in Japan. However, the demand for non-Japanese stocks by Japanese investors has not been large, even when the stock market was at its peak in the late 1980s.

Hong Kong Stock Exchange

The Hong Kong Stock Exchange is the second largest stock exchange in Asia. The exchange was merged in 2000 with the Hong Kong futures exchange and the Hong Kong clearing corporation to create Hong Kong Exchanges and Clearing Limited (HKEx).

The regulator for stock exchange listings is the Securities and Futures Commission, although day-to-day administration of listing matters is delegated to the exchange.

The exchange has an electronic trading system that is accessible only to exchange participants. Investors wishing to buy or sell shares must go through a broker who is an exchange participant. As in Tokyo, trading is on a board lot system, with the size of a board lot unit of shares depending on the price per share. On receiving an order from a client, the broker, an exchange participant, enters the details into an Automatic Order Matching and Execution System (AMS) that is an electronic order book-trading system.

Most trades are cash-settled, on T + 2. However, there are facilities for trading shares on credit, whereby investors do not settle immediately but are given some credit by their broker. When trading is on a credit system investors are required to provide some margin as a deposit to cover possible losses, and to protect the exchange from credit risk.

As in Japan, securities traditionally have been in certificate form, but certificates have been immobilized in a central depository, and shares are held in electronic form and transferred by book entry. The clearing corporation provides a central clearing and settlement system for transactions on both the stock exchange and the futures exchange.

Germany: the Deutsche Börse

The Deutsche Börse is the holding company for Germany's stock exchanges and futures exchange (Eurex). Germany has eight stock exchanges, of which Frankfurt is the largest and most important. The others are Berlin, Bremen, Düsseldorf, Hamburg, Hanover, Munich and Stuttgart.

The market is divided into four segments, the most important is the main segment, or Amtlicher Handel, that is the segment for shares of the largest companies. There is also a Neuer Markt, established successfully in 1997, for shares in young and rapidly growing high-tech companies, such as companies in the telecommunications and multimedia industries.

The Deutsche Börse has expanded rapidly in recent years, and has relied for its growth on the use of technology for trading and settlement systems. Although some floor trading is still conducted in the exchanges, most trading in shares is now conducted through Xetra, an electronic trading system, that was introduced in 1997. Most Xetra terminals are in Germany, but some dealers outside Germany have terminals and use the system for dealing. All shares listed on the Frankfurt exchange, including shares of Neuer Markt companies, can be traded on Xetra that uses a system of designated sponsors, a form of market maker, who quote firm bid and offer prices in shares of specific companies. Designated sponsors help to maintain a liquid secondary market in the shares.

Share transactions are cleared and settled through Clearstream, an organization created in 2000 through the merger of Deutsche Börse Clearing and Cedel, the international central securities depository.

France: the Paris Bourse

The major stock exchange in France is the Pairs Bourse. This merged with the Brussels and Amsterdam exchanges in 2000 to create the Euronext exchange, but still retains its own identity. The government's market watchdog for the French stock market is the Commission des Opérations be Bourse, or COB.

French equities are of three types:

- bearer (porteur)
- registered (nominatif), and
- identifiable bearer (titre au porteur identifiable, or TPI).

Despite their name, TPI shares are a form of registered shares.

All types of share are held in book-entry form, and share transfers are by book entry. Most share certificates were abolished as long ago as 1984.

The trading system has been computerized since 1987 on a trading system known as cotation assisté en continue (CAC). This is an order-driven electronic order-book system. Investors wishing to buy or sell shares will go through a broker (an order collector) or directly through a trading member of the exchange.

There are three segments to the market, the premier marché for shares in the largest companies, the second marché for shares in medium-sized companies, and a nouveau marché for shares in younger companies, set up in 1996.

Transactions in most shares on the premier marché is on the last trading day of the month in which the transaction is made. This monthly settlement basis is called règlement mensuel. Transactions in other shares are on a cash basis, and settlement is on T + 3.

Clearing and settlement of transactions is the responsibility of Clearnet, a wholly owned subsidiary of the Bourse that operates a central counterparty settlement system called Relit.

International Equities

An international equity issue is an issue of shares that is placed simultaneously with investors in several different countries. An international issue might be made at the same time as a domestic issue, or at the same time as a public issue in another domestic equity market. For example, a UK company wanting to make a large equity issue might arrange simultaneously:

- a public offering in the UK
- the placement of an international tranche of the shares in several countries in Europe, and
- an ADR issue in the US, either as a public issue with a NYSE or Nasdaq listing, or in the private placement market.

An attraction of an international equity issue is that a company can widen its shareholder base and encourage investment in it shares by more foreign investors. This helps to give the company and its shares a higher international profile, and also might boost the market price through greater demand.

However, a major problem with international equity issues is ensuring that the shares placed in another country remain with investors in that country, and do not find their way back to the company's domestic stock market. For example, suppose that a UK company makes an international issue of new shares in the same class and ranking equally with shares already in issue. The shares might be sold to investors in France, Germany and Spain. After the issue, when investors in those countries want to sell their shares in a secondary market, there is a strong possibility that they will be sold on the London Stock Exchange, and be purchased by UK investors. If so, the company's international investor base will shrink in size.

It is important to companies as well as to foreign investors that there should be an active and liquid secondary market in international equities. The lead manager for an international issue, and possibly other banks too, usually will give an undertaking to provide a secondary market in the shares after the issue.

A feature of international equities is that:

- when the shares are issued, they are listed in at least one country, and admitted to trading on the stock exchange of that country, but
- trading in the international tranche of the share issue will be organized largely by member firms of ISMA, rather than conducted through the stock exchange trading system.

The secondary share market in international equities and bonds is self-regulated, and market practise regulations are the responsibility of ISMA. Many transactions are still made by phone, and so the market is largely an over-the-counter market. However, ISMA provides its members with:

- Trax, an order-matching and trade-reporting system, and
- Coredeal, an electronic order dealing system.

Trax serves two functions:

- Transactions in international securities can be matched and confirmed, both parties entering trade details into the system that matches them automatically or highlights non-matches for the parties concerned to sort out the discrepancy. Electronic order matching and confirmation is particularly important in international dealing because the risks of misunderstandings between buyer and seller are greater. An automated matching system is faster and more efficient.
- The regulatory authorities or stock exchanges of the country of a buyer and seller may impose regulations about the reporting of transactions in securities, including transactions in listed securities that are traded off the exchange. Trax provides a regulatory order-reporting system whereby details of transactions are sent to the appropriate regulatory body or exchange automatically.

Although much trading in international securities is by phone, ISMA has set up Coredeal, an electronic order-driven trading system, and expects that a large proportion of trading will switch to this system.

Summary

Trading and clearing and settlement systems vary between countries and markets but many have essentially similar characteristics.

- Major stock exchanges provide an electronic trading system, at least for the shares of the largest companies. Electronic systems can be either order-driven, using an electronic order book, or quote-driven.
- Markets provide for securities to be held in dematerialized form with a national or international central securities depository. A CSD arranges for stock transfers to be made by book entry, and most CSDs can provide for delivery versus payment settlement of share transactions.
- Many exchanges guarantee settlement of transactions by arranging for an agent organization to act as a central counterparty.
- A central counterparty arrangement makes possible the settlement of transactions with brokers and large investment institutions by means of a single net payment each day.

As trading systems and clearing and settlement systems become computerized and more efficient, it seems likely that future trends in the market will include:

- movement towards a shorter settlement cycle from the T + 3 applied in most leading markets, and
- alliances, possibly mergers, between stock exchanges or stock-markets as global investors demand simpler systems for trading globally in securities.

8

Stock Market Indices

A stock market index is a share-price index based on the average price for a basket of shares that are traded on the market. The shares in the basket or portfolio should be representative of the market as a whole, but need not contain shares of all the companies traded on the market.

A base date is selected when the index is typically set at a level of either 100 or 1,000. As share prices rise or fall, the average value of the shares in the representative basket or portfolio also will rise or fall, and the index will go up or down accordingly. A rise or fall in the index ought to give a reliable indication of share price rises or falls in the market taken as a whole.

In every stock market, there is at least one reported price index for shares in the major companies traded on the market, or for shares in all or most of the companies traded on the market, an all-share index.

Increasingly investment is global. Investment institutions in countries such as the US and UK maintain investment portfolios in all the major international companies, and in companies in different countries around the world. To meet the requirements of global investors, stock-price indices also are produced for:

- shares in companies in a particular geographical region of the world such as Europe, Latin America or the Asia Pacific region
- a selection of international companies, whose shares are traded on different stock markets.

Why are Stock Market Indices Needed?

A stock market index condenses information about share prices in the market, or in a sector of the market, into a simple and easy-to-follow figure. This helps investors and market analysts to assess the price performance of shares, and perhaps to predict future share price movements.

Movements in a stock market's main index generally are taken as a guide to current market sentiment. A rise or fall in the index in one market can affect sentiment in another market. This often has been the case between the US and UK, where an upward or downward movement in the Dow Jones Industrial Average index in New York is often followed the next day by a similar movement in the FTSE All-Share Index and FTSE 100 index in London.

A stock market index has several possible uses.

- Changes in the price of an individual stock can be compared with changes in the index for the market as a whole or the index for a particular sector of the market, to judge whether it is outperforming or underperforming the market.
- The price performance of different sectors of the market can be compared to judge which sector is a more profitable area for investment.
- The price performance of large and small companies can be compared. For many markets, a small companies share-price index, or small cap index, is compiled.
- The price performance of the stock markets in different countries can be compared.

Tracker Funds: Passive and Active Fund Management

Stock market indices are of great significance to investment institutions and their fund managers.

A tracker fund is an investment fund, such as a pension fund, that holds a portfolio of investments that are intended to follow or track the average returns from a particular stock market. The investments in the portfolio of the fund should be comparable with the portfolio of shares that make up the stock market index. Creating and running a tracker fund is passive fund management because the fund manager does not have to select individual stocks in which to invest that he/she thinks will do well. Rather, he/she simply must maintain a portfolio of investments that track the market.

The managers of tracker funds will have to check that the returns from their portfolio of investments have achieved the same returns as the market as a whole. Returns are measured by the rise or fall in the index over time, plus dividends or interest. Statistics also are produced for the average dividend yield for the market as a whole over a given period of time. A fund tracking the Standard & Poor's 500 Index should achieve returns that are reflected by the performance of the index over time.

An active investment fund is one whose manager tries to identify stocks that will outperform the market. The performance of an active fund can be measured against the stock market as a whole, against the market index. For example, suppose that an investment fund specializes in UK shares. Investors in the fund would expect the returns from the fund to exceed the market average returns, measured perhaps by the performance of the FTSE All-Share Index.

Equity Derivatives

Some derivative instruments are traded by futures and options exchanges where the underlying item being traded is a portfolio of shares represented by a stock market index. Equity index futures and equity index options are explained in the next chapter.

Methods of Calculating a Price Index

A price index can be calculated in several ways. Without going into excessive detail, it is useful to be aware that:

- an index can be based on either an arithmetic or a geometric average of share prices, and
- an index also can be either an unweighted or a weighted

average. A weighted index is sometimes called a capitalization-weighted index.

Stock market indices may be based on a weighted or an unweighted average, and on an arithmetical or a geometric average.

Example
A small stock market consists of shares in just three companies, Alpha, Beta and Gamma. The total shares in issue, and their prices, are as follows.

	Number of shares	Price per share
Alpha	5 million	100
Beta	1 million	200
Gamma	2 million	150

Analysis
The average share price can be calculated in any of the following ways.

An unweighted arithmetical average is the simple average of all the shares, calculated by totalling the price of one share for each company in the index, and dividing by the number of companies.

$$\frac{100 + 200 + 150}{3} = 150$$

An unweighted geometrical average is found by multiplying with each other the price per share for each share in the index, and then taking the nth root, where n is the number of shares in the index. In this example, because there are just three stocks in the index, we take the cube root.

$$\sqrt[3]{100 \times 200 \times 150} = 144.2$$

A weighted average arithmetical average takes into account the number of shares in issue for each company, and so reflects the market capitalization of the companies whose shares make up the index. This means, for example, that if Company A has twice as many shares listed as Company B, and their share price is exactly the same, Company A shares will be given twice as much weight in the index as Company B shares. In this example, the weighted average price is as follows:

	Number of shares (A)	Price per share (B)	Weighted total (A) x (B)
Alpha	5 million	100	500 million
Beta	1 million	200	200 million
Gamma	2 million	150	300 million
Total	8 million		1,000 million

$$\text{Weighted average price} = \frac{1{,}000 \text{ million}}{8 \text{ million}} = 125.0$$

A *weighted average geometric index* also takes into account the number of shares in issue as well as the price per share. In this example, it is:

$$\sqrt[8]{(100)^5 \times (200)^1 \times (150)^2} = 120.7$$

The average price at a given reference date is given an index value of 100 or 1,000, and subsequent changes in the average price can be indexed accordingly. Using the above example, suppose the weighted average arithmetic average of 125 is taken as the base for the index, and given an index value of 1,000. If the average share price subsequently rises to 128, the index will rise from 1,000 to 1,024 (1,000 x 128/125), a rise of 24 points.

Shares that are not Traded

A problem with deciding weightings for a weighted average price index can be listed stocks that are not actively traded. For example, suppose that Zeta is a listed company whose shares are traded on a stock market, but that Zeta is 75% owned by a larger company, Omega Corporation, that regards its shareholding in Zeta as a long-term investment. If Zeta has 400 million shares in issue, a problem for the constructors of the stock market index is whether to give Zeta a weighting of 400 million shares, the total listed, or just 100 million shares, the total that is available for active trading. A problem with using the full total of 400 million shares is that tracker funds will be required to invest in a quantity of Zeta shares that reflects this weighting in the index. If only 100 million shares are available for trading, the competition between funds for the relatively limited number of shares might drive up the share price to an unreasonable level, and effectively distort the index.

Adjustments to an Index: Changes in the Index Constituents
Adjustments are made continually to a share-price index, particularly a capitalization-weighted index, to allow for changes such as:

- new issues of shares by companies
- takeovers of companies in the index, either by another company in the index or by another company, for example a foreign company, and a subsequent de-listing of the shares
- companies going into liquidation
- in the case of an index for the largest companies in a stock market, such as the FTSE 100 in the UK, some companies dropping out of the top league and being replaced by others.

Stock Exchange Indices, Sector Indices, Regional Indices and World Indices

A large range of share-price indices are produced by different organizations to meet the requirements of clients such as stock markets and institutional investors. The leading providers of indices include Morgan Stanley Capital International (MSCI), Dow Jones & Company, FTSE International and Standard & Poor's Corporation. These organizations compete for business. For example, an index producer might produce a cross-border index and persuade investment institutions to set up tracker funds to track the index.

Indices might be provided as end-of-day indices that are computed at the end of trading each day and based on closing prices of stocks. Alternatively, users may prefer real-time indices, where the index is continually updated throughout the day as share prices in the market fluctuate.

National Stock Markets
The first stock market indices were indices for a particular stock exchange. The Dow Jones Industrial Average is an index of 30 stocks on the New York Stock Exchange and dates back to 1896.

US Market Indices

Every major stock market has a stock market index. The most widely reported in the US are the following:

- the Dow Jones Industrial Average
- Standard & Poor's 500
- the NYSE Composite
- the Nasdaq 100
- the Amex Market Value Index.

The most widely reported index for the US is the Dow Jones Industrial Average (DJIA), produced by Dow Jones & Company. This is an unweighted index of prices for 30 leading blue-chip companies whose shares are traded on the New York Stock Exchange. Despite being an unweighted index of just 30 stocks, the DJIA has proved itself to be a reliable indicator of general price movements on the NYSE. Dow Jones also publishes an index of transport company stocks and an index of stock prices for the utilities industries.

Standard & Poor's produces a number of capitalization-weighted indices for major US stocks, listed on various stock markets. The most widely reported of these is a 500-stock composite index, the S & P 500. There is also an S & P 100 index for the top 100 companies. In addition, Standard & Poor's publishes separate indices for industrial sectors.

UK Market Indices

For each stock exchange, there will be a number of different indices. The FTSE indices are typical of this. FTSE International provides the main stock market indices for shares traded on the London Stock Exchange. These indices are calculated according to ground rules established by the London Stock Exchange and the *Financial Times,* with the assistance of the Institute of Actuaries and the Faculty of Actuaries. The indices are based on weighted arithmetical averages of share prices. They are produced by an organization called FTSE International that is owned partly by the London Stock Exchange and partly by the *Financial Times.*

The FTSE indices include the following:

- The FTSE 100, known colloquially as the Footsie, that is based on a weighted average price for the shares of the 100 largest domestic companies by market capitalization. The base date is January 3rd 1984, when the index was set at 1,000. Trading on the London Stock Exchange consists mainly of shares within the FTSE 100 that is the most widely reported index, and the index on which equity futures and options for the UK stock market are based.
- The FTSE 250 is an index for the next 250 largest domestic companies on the London Stock Exchange. This was devised in response to demand for an index to monitor the performance of the next largest companies on the market.
- The FTSE 350 is a combined index for the top 350 companies whose shares make up the FTSE 100 and FTSE 250.
- The FTSE SmallCap is an index, as its name suggests, for the smallest companies whose shares are traded on the London main market.
- The FTSE AIM index is an index of prices for shares traded on the Alternative Investment Market.
- The FTSE All-Share Index is an index that reflects the current share prices of most, but not all, domestic companies whose shares are traded on the main London market. Although the FTSE 100 is the most widely reported UK index, the All-Share index usually is regarded as a yardstick for judging the investment performance of fund managers because the index is more representative of the London market as a whole.

Other National Market Indices

Other widely reported national market indices include:

- the Nikkei 225 for the Tokyo Stock Exchange
- the DAX for the German stock markets
- the CAC 40 for the Paris Bourse, although an index has been established for the Euronext exchange, of which the Paris Bourse is a part
- the Hang Seng Index for Hong Kong.

Sector Indices

An all-share index can be broken down into separate indices for industry sectors. These can be used as yardsticks for measuring the performance of individual companies against the stock market as a whole, and against the performance of the sector to which they belong. They can be used to compare the performance of one industrial sector against another also.

FTSE International provides the following sector classifications for the London market.

Financials	Banks
	Insurance
	Life assurance
	Investment companies
	Real estate
	Speciality and other finance
Non-financials	
Resources	Mining
	Oil and gas
Basic industries	Chemicals
	Construction and building materials
	Forestry and paper
	Steel and other metals
General industrials	Aerospace and defense
	Electronic and electrical equipment
	Engineering and machinery
Cyclical consumer goods	Automobiles and parts
	Household goods and textiles
Non-cyclical consumer goods	Beverages
	Food producers and processors
	Health
	Packaging
	Personal care and house products
	Pharmaceuticals
	Tobacco

Cyclical services	Distributors
	General retailers
	Leisure, entertainment and hotels
	Media and photography
	Support services
	Transport
Non-cyclical services	Food and drug retailers
	Telecommunication services
Utilities	Electricity
	Gas distribution
	Water
Information technology	Information technology hardware
	Software and computer services

World Indices and Regional Indices

Fund managers invest in companies around the world and have to monitor the performance of the markets they have chosen for investment. Investment organizations often focus on investments in a particular region of the world such as the Pacific Basin, Latin America or Europe. Consequently, it could be important to judge whether an institution should have invested more heavily in Europe and less in the Pacific Basin. Alternatively, a fund manager may wish to compare the performance of his regional fund against the average performance of share investments for the region.

To meet such demands several indices have been produced by organizations such as MSCI and FTSE International to monitor share prices in different parts of the world using indices that have been constructed using the same method. A world index can be constructed from the sub-indices of different countries, and indices for different regions of the world also can be constructed.

Sub-sets of the MSCI World Index include:

- a North American Index
- the Europe, Australia, New Zealand and Far East (EAFE) Index
- a Europe 13 Index

- a Nordic countries Index
- a Pacific and Far East Index.

A problem for world indices and cross-border indices is the choice of currency of measurement. To bring shares into a common index, they must be valued in the same currency. An index might perform better in one currency, in terms of return on investment, than in terms of another currency, depending on changes in the value of the measuring currency against other currencies in which the various shares are actually priced.

World indices are computed in several currencies, but the most widely publicised are those with dollars as the measuring currency such as the MSCI and the FTSE World Indices.

Cross-Border Funds

Some investors choose to hold a portfolio of major international companies, rather than a general portfolio of shares for a country or a particular region. For such investors a number of cross-border stock market indices have been developed where the focus is on the particular companies. Indices of this type include:

- the DJ Stoxx 50 and the DJ Stoxx Euro 50
- the FTSE Eurotop 100, FTSE Eurotop 300, FTSE Multinationals and FTSE Global 100 indices
- stock market indices for emerging markets generally, without any particular regional focus.

The Dow Jones Stoxx indices are produced by an index provider (Stoxx), as a collaboration between Dow Jones, the Deutsche Börse, the Paris bourse and the Swiss stock exchange. The DJ Stoxx 50 is an index of shares in the top 50 companies in Europe, and the DJ Euro Stoxx 50 is an index of 50 top companies in the euro zone.

Measuring Performance with Indices

A particular use for a share-price index is monitoring the performance of an investment fund or investment portfolio.

Example

An investment fund manager is assessing the performance of the shares in UK equities fund for the past 12 months. The market value of the fund a year ago was £747.2 million exactly, and it is now £800 million exactly. The dividend yield on the shares in the fund averaged 2.5% for the year, based on end-of-year, current share values.

During the same period, the FTSE All-Share Index, against which the fund manager measures his/her performance, rose from 3140 to 3345, and the average dividend yield from shares in this index was 2.2%.

Analysis

The return from the equity fund, consisting of price growth plus dividend yield, can be compared with the average returns from investing in the All-Share Index. This is the return that the fund manager would have obtained by investing in a weighted basket of shares of the FTSE All-Share Index.

	Equity fund	**FTSE All-Share**
Current value	£800.0 million	3345
Value 12 months ago	£747.2 million	3140
Increase in value	£52.8 million	205
Price increase as a % of current value	6.6%	6.1%
Dividend yield	2.5%	2.2%
Total return	9.1%	8.3%

The fund outperformed the All-Share Index by 0.8%.

9

Stock Options and Futures

Traded stock options and stock index options, and equity futures are capital market derivative instruments. They are not sources of equity capital for companies, and are not issued by companies. However, they provide investors with readily available opportunities to manage their investment risk, either to reduce the risk of adverse price movements on securities in their investment portfolio, or to speculate on favorable price movements for a relatively small investment outlay.

This chapter explains five types of instrument, all traded on stock exchanges, options exchanges, or futures and options exchanges. These are:

- stock options (traded share options)
- stock index options
- stock index futures
- options on stock index futures
- futures on the shares of individual companies.

Options

An option gives its holder the right but not the obligation to buy or sell an item at a fixed price on or before a fixed future date.

An option to buy the item at a fixed price is a call option, and an option to sell at a fixed price is a put option. The fixed price is called the strike price or exercise price.

A call option or put option is purchased from a seller, who either creates the option (writes the option) or sells an option in a secondary market.

Options that are listed on and traded through a recognized exchange are called traded options. Traded options can be sold before their maturity or expiry/exercise date, through the exchange. At any time, a number of options will be traded for the same item, i.e. with different exercise prices and different expiry dates.

Traded Stock Options (Share Options)

A traded stock option or traded share option is a contract that gives its holder the right but not the obligation to buy or sell – call or put options – a quantity of shares in a company at a specified price, on or before a given date. After this date, the option ceases to exist.

- If a call option is exercised, at the holder's request, the seller of the option is obliged to sell the underlying shares to the option holder at the specified price.
- If a put option is exercised, at the holder's request, the seller of the option is obliged to buy the underlying shares from the option holder at the specified price.

A call-option holder will exercise his/her option to buy at the strike price if the market price of the shares rises above the strike price, seeking to benefit from a rise in the share price. Similarly, a put option holder will exercise his/her option to sell at the strike price if the market price of the shares falls below the strike price, seeking to benefit from a fall in the share price.

- The maximum investment risk for the buyer of an option is its purchase cost, the premium. If the option is not exercised, the option holder has lost his investment in full. This is the risk that the buyer of an option must set against the prospect of making a profit if the share price moves favorably and the option is exercised.
- In contrast, the maximum gain that the seller of an option can

make is the income from the sale of the option. If the option is not exercised, the option writer has no obligations to the option holder, and receives the premium in full. On the other hand, if the share price moves in the option holder's favor, and the option is exercised, the option writer stands to make a loss.

In the US, stock options are traded on several exchanges, of which the Chicago Board Options Exchange (CBOE) is the largest. All stock options traded on US exchanges are guaranteed and cleared by The Options Clearing Corporation (OCC), a registered clearing corporation with the Securities and Exchange Commission. The OCC becomes the central counterparty to each transaction, and becomes the buyer to every seller of options and the seller to every buyer of options. In the UK, stock options (share options) are traded on the London International Financial Futures Exchange (LIFFE) for shares of about 80 – 90 large companies.

Stock option contracts are standardized.

- They are for a standard quantity of underlying shares in a particular company, 100 shares in the case of US stock options and 1,000 shares in the case of most UK traded share options.
- They have a standard expiry date. Options on an exchange are issued in series, with a series expiring every month or every three months. At any time, there will be trading in options with three or four future expiry dates up to twelve months ahead. Option holders can exercise their options, or close their position in options at any time up to the expiry date.
- The exercise prices (strike prices) at which options can be written are determined by the exchange. Options are traded at strike prices a little above and below the current market price.

Options are described by the name of the company, the strike price and the expiry date. If there are traded options in PQR Corporation on CBOE, for example, a PQR July 50 call would be a call option on 100 shares in PQR Corporation at a strike price of $50 per share, and an expiry date in July.

Call and put options are bought and sold on the exchange, at prices (premiums) set by supply and demand between sellers and buyers. Premiums are quoted in dollars per option on US exchanges. If the premium on a PQR 250 July call is 2½, the cost of buying an option on 100 shares would be $250.

In the US, the buyer of an option must pay the OCC the full price of the option on purchase if the expiry date is within the next nine months. The writer of the option does not receive the payment of the premium, however. On the contrary, the option writer is required to leave the premium with the OCC and in addition provide further margin to cover the possibility of making a loss on his/her trading position.

The Price of Options

The purchase price of an option is called its premium. The size of the premium for an option depends on several factors. These include:

- the difference between the exercise price and the current share price, the intrinsic value of the option. The premium for an in-the-money option must be at least the difference between the exercise price and the current market price of the share, but will in fact be more unless the option is reaching its expiry
- the length of time remaining to the expiry date
- the volatility of the share price, or stock index, in the case of stock index options.

The price of an option will be higher for more distant expiry dates, and options are said to have a time value that is reflected in the premium. When an option has a fairly long time remaining before expiry and the share price is volatile, the premium will be higher than for an option with a short term before expiry where the underlying shares have a fairly stable share price. There is a greater chance with a long-dated option that the share price will move in the option-holder's favor and against the option seller.

Dealing

There are two parties to each traded option contract, the seller (writer) and the buyer (holder). An investor wishing to write options or buy options may do so through a member firm of an exchange.

- An investor who buys options without previously having sold options in the same series, is said to take a long position in the option.
- An investor who sells options without previously having bought options in the same series, is said to take a short position in the option.

On or before the expiry of an option, the option holder may exercise the option. A call option holder will exercise his/her right to buy 1,000 shares at the exercise price, and could then resell the shares immediately in the market to make a profit. The seller of the share option must supply the shares and, if necessary, would have to buy the shares in the stock market and resell them to the option holder at a loss. In practise, the clearing house acting for an exchange acts as a central counterparty for all transactions, but when an option is exercised by a holder, the clearing house will nominate an option writer who must deliver the shares.

Similarly, if the holder of a put option exercises the option, he/she will sell 1,000 shares at the exercise price, and the option writer will be required to buy them at that price.

Closing a Position

Instead of exercising an option, a holder can close his/her position before expiry. However, very few option contracts are exercised, and most positions are closed before expiry at a profit or loss.

- An option holder, an investor with a long position, can close a position by selling an equal number of option contracts in the same series. The profit or loss on option dealing will be the difference between the price paid for the options originally, and the selling price on closing the position.
- An option writer, an investor with a short position, can close a position by buying an equal number of option contracts in the

same series. The profit or loss on option dealing will be the difference between the price received for the options originally and the price paid for buying the options to close the position.

Closing a position before expiry gives the investor flexibility as to timing. A position can be closed at any time. In addition, the gain or loss on the option dealing is realized in cash, without any requirement to buy or sell shares.

Example
An investor believes that the price of shares in XYZ Corporation will rise, and in February buys 40 July call options at an exercise price of 420¢. The option premium for the purchase is 35¢.

In mid-April, the share price has risen to 427¢, and the investor closes his/her position by selling 40 July 420 contracts at 41¢.

Analysis
The investor makes a profit on closing his/her position. The profit is 6¢ per share, the difference in premium at which he/she bought (35¢) and the selling price (41¢). Each option is for 1,000 shares, and because he/she bought and sold 40 contracts, the total profit is $2,400 (1,000 shares x 6¢ x 40 contracts).

The original outlay was $14,000 (1,000 shares x 35¢ x 40 contracts). Therefore there is a profit of over 17% on the original investment. If shares in XYZ had been bought at 420¢, instead of buying options at 35¢, the total investment would have been $168,000 (40,000 shares at 420¢) and the profit would have been 7¢ per share, or $2,800 in total, giving a return of just 1.7% on the investment.

Using Stock Options
Stock options can be used by investors either as a protection against an adverse movement in the share price, or to speculate on a company's share-price movement. Their most common use is for speculation because the potential return as a percentage of the initial investment, is higher for options than for the shares. This is because the initial outlay is

much lower: a premium to purchase an option is less than the cost of buying the underlying shares.

Stock Index Options

A stock index or share-price index measures the price movement in an underlying basket or portfolio of shares. Traded options are available on share price indices; for example options traded on CBOE include options on the Standard & Poor's 100, Standard & Poor's 500 and Nasdaq 100 indices. Similar share-price index options are traded on other exchanges in the US and around the world.

Index options can be useful to an investor either for speculative purposes or as a hedge against risk of adverse movements in market prices generally.

The most heavily traded stock index option is the CBOE's option on the S & P 100 index. For these options, strike price intervals are just five index points. Premiums are quoted in dollars, to fractions of one-eighth of a dollar and sometimes to sixteenths of a dollar. The purchase price of an option is the premium multiplied by 100. For example, an investor buying S & P 100 options at 2½ would pay $250 per contract.

Example 1
An investor is convinced that the stock market is set to rise, but is not confident about any specific individual stock and does not have sufficient funds to acquire a well-diversified equity portfolio. The investor decides to buy options that hopefully will rise in value with the market. The DJIA stands at 6289. The investor buys ten April 6400 call contracts at 141¢, paying $14,100 in total (1,000 x 141¢ per contract, x 10 contracts). The DJIA rises to 6480, and the investor is able to sell the contracts at 186¢ or $18,600 in total, giving a profit before expenses of $4,500. The return on the initial investment is 4,500/14,100, or nearly 32%.

Example 2

An investor bought 100,000 shares in Able Inc, a company in which traded options are not available, at a price of 260¢, when the DJIA was 6500. The investor was convinced that Able would outperform the market but was worried that share prices in general would fall. It was decided to buy four 6500 put options at a price of 190¢, at a cost of $7,600 (4 x 1,000 x 190¢).

The four options were bought because the shares in Able were worth $260,000 (100,000 x 260¢). The nominal value of one option contract is $65,000 when the DJIA is 6500. Four contracts have a nominal value of $260,000, the same value as the shares in Able.

Some time later the investor's fears are justified. The index fell to 5850, a 10% fall, and the price of Able fell less steeply, to 247¢, a 5% fall.

Analysis

The share price of Able has fallen less than the market average, but without the options the investor would still have lost $13,000 (100,000 shares x the fall in share price of 13¢). Suppose, however, that the investor can sell the four options at 690¢. The overall position will be as follows:

	$	$
Loss in value of Able shares		- 13,000
Cost of index options purchased	- 7,600	
Income from options sold (4 x 1000 x 690¢)	27,600	
Gain on options		20,000
		7,000

The investor has managed to offset the loss on the shares with the profit on the options trading.

Stock Index Futures

Futures contracts are traded in a number of stock indices including:

- the S & P 500
- the Nasdaq 100
- the FTSE 100
- the Nikkei 225
- the Hang Seng
- the DAX

Each futures exchange trades its own futures contracts. The Chicago Mercantile Exchange (CME) trades futures in the S & P 500 and the Nasdaq 100. LIFFE trades futures in the FTSE 100.

Features of a Stock Index Futures Contract

A financial futures contract is a standard, exchange-traded contract to buy/sell a standard quantity of a particular financial instrument at a specified date in the future, at a price agreed between the buyer and seller when the contract is made. A future is a type of forward contract, bought and sold through a futures exchange.

Unlike option, where the option buyer can choose whether or not to exercise an option, both parties to a futures contract incur obligations. If either party holds his/her position in the futures to maturity, his/her side of the transaction must be completed.

A stock index futures contract is an agreement for the purchase and sale of a portfolio of shares, represented by the named share price index, at a specified price, the stock index level, and on a specified future date. For example, suppose a FTSE 100 September futures contract is sold at a price of 6415. The buyer and seller would be agreeing to exchange the underlying portfolio of shares for settlement in September at a price represented by a FTSE 100 Index level of 6415.

Underlying Share Value

There is a standard quantity of underlying shares for each futures contract. For the S & P 500 contract, the current value of the underlying shares is found by multiplying the futures price, i.e. the S & P 500 index, by $250. If the futures price is 1400, the value of the shares represented by the futures contract would be $350,000 ($250 x 1400).

Similarly, with the FTSE 100 futures contract on LIFFE, the current value of the underlying shares is £10 per index point. If the FTSE 100 index stands at 6600, for example, the value of the shares represented by the futures contract would be £66,000 (6600 x £10).

Futures contracts have standard delivery dates each year, contracts for settlement being in March, June, September and December.

The price at which futures are bought and sold is determined by supply and demand in the market. US futures exchanges still have floor trading, dealing on the trading floor of the exchange, but most other futures exchanges around the world now trade by means of an electronic dealing system. Every futures exchange guarantees performance of contracts. A clearing house acting on behalf of the exchange becomes the counterparty to every buyer and seller. For example, if Alpha sells 40 stock index futures to Beta, the clearing house will become the buyer of the 40 contracts from Alpha and also will become the seller of the 40 contracts to Beta.

Margins (Performance Bond)

A futures contract is a contract to buy or sell at a future date, and the buyer does not pay the seller anything when the contract is agreed. Payment will occur only at settlement date unless the buyer and seller have each closed their futures position before then. However, as a protection against credit risk, i.e. non-performance of the contract, the buyer and seller must pay a returnable cash deposit to the futures exchange. This deposit is called a margin or performance bond. Additional deposits, known as variation margins, will be called from the buyer or seller if the index price moves unfavorably – down in the case of the buyer or up in the case of the seller.

Closing a Futures Position

A futures contract, unlike a share option, creates a binding obligation on both the buyer and the seller. However, it is usual to close a futures position before settlement date and most contracts do not run to completion.

- A seller of futures contracts who has a short position in the futures, can close his/her position by purchasing an equal number of matching contracts for the same settlement date before the settlement date is reached.
- A buyer of futures contracts who has a long position, can close his/her position by selling an equal number of matching contracts before the settlement date.

When a position is closed, the investor makes a profit or loss from the difference between the buying and selling prices. The size of the profit or loss will depend on the change in the stock index between the purchase and sale dates or sale and purchase dates. This is because the futures price should rise or fall with rises or falls in the underlying stock index.

Profits or Losses on Futures Positions

The profits or losses on futures positions are monitored daily. Movements in the stock index are measured in ticks, a tick is the minimum movement in the price. For an S & P 500 futures contract a tick is a 0.1 change in the index, and a rise or fall of one tick has a value of $25. This is because each index point is worth $250, and a change in the index by 0.1 has a value of $25 because $250 x 0.1 = $25.

Similarly with the FTSE 100 contract, a tick is 0.5 and this has a value of £5 (£10 per index point x 0.5).

Example

Beta purchases 20 FTSE 100 September futures contracts at a price of 6700 in July and sells 20 September contracts in August when the price has risen to 6780.

Analysis

Beta has made a gain of 80 index points or 160 ticks per contract, and the profit is £16,000, 80 x £10 or 160 x £5 per contract, multiplied by 20 contracts.

Using Stock Index Futures

Stock index futures can be used by investors to hedge against a fall in the value of their share portfolio or to speculate for a relatively low cash outlay, on a rise or fall in stock market prices.

- A speculator who expects the stock market to rise can buy stock index futures, and hope to sell matching futures at a later date at a higher price.
- A speculator expecting a fall in prices can sell stock index futures, and hope to close the position before settlement date by purchasing a matching contract at a lower price.

Options on Stock Index Futures

Options on stock index futures are options contracts giving their holder the right, but not the obligation, to buy (call option) or sell (put option) a stock index futures contract at a specified price on or before a specified date.

These are traded on the same exchanges that trade the futures contract, and give investors further flexibility for hedging against the risk of a fall in share prices, or for speculating in rises or falls in share prices.

Futures on the Shares of Individual Companies (Universal Stock Futures)

In January 2001, LIFFE introduced futures contracts on the shares of some individual companies. The companies for which there are share futures, called universal stock futures by the exchange, include companies from the US, the UK and continental Europe. The underlying contract is for 100 shares in the company, in the case of US and continental European companies, and 1,000 shares in the case of UK companies. Futures are priced in dollars (US companies), pence (UK companies) or euros (continental European companies), and the minimum price movement in the contracts is $0.01, 0.5 pence, or 0.01 euros.

Program Trading

For a time in the late 1980s, following the collapse in share prices in October 1987, investor confidence in equities was weak. Share price volatility at this time was made worse by program trading and arbitrage in stock index futures and options.

Program trading means that the purchase or sale of stock index futures or options by an investment institution is automatically triggered by computer when the index breaches a pre-established level. When several institutions start to buy or sell simultaneously, this can cause large rises or falls in share prices and the index of share prices. There have been some attempts to discourage program trading, and each futures exchange has rules for halting trading when prices move by more than a certain amount within a given period of time. However, program trading is still used by investment institutions.

Conclusion

Options and futures are instruments for investment management, rather than securities issued to raise capital. Nevertheless, they are important to the development of the capital markets because they give greater flexibility to investors, and thus make the capital markets more attractive to them.

Index